DR. MARTIN ELLIS JR.

The Kingdom Perspective

It's All About The Kingdom

GLORY RELEASE GLOBAL

I dedicate this book to the following:

To my children: Byron, Remani, Martrice, Zipporah, Marquise, Marnae, Martin-Elias, & Uriah, I love you all very much. The KINGDOM Perspective transcends all generations. I pray that the KINGDOM overtake you all and your generations after you. My hope is that you find your KINGDOM purpose and yield all to the King of Kings.

To the youth generations and the generations to come, may you catch the rhythm of the KINGDOM of God and advance the KINGDOM.

Contents

Preface

In the year 1997, I had an encounter with the Lord that impacted me so that it set me in a journey that I am still on this very day. In this encounter, it was revealed on a high level what my call and destiny was and what areas I should focus on when it comes to teaching and preaching. In context of this book, I was shown that my mandate and call was to equip a people in the areas of grace, the glory, and the KINGDOM of God.

This led me to seek the Word of God and the Lord immediately thinking that I was supposed to be on the forefront and right away. But there was still so much processing that I had to go through. For over 25 years, I have made mistakes, had ups and downs, and at times went in circles in the wilderness. As the years went on, I am now just seeing that everything was for this season to be a sent one of the KINGDOM to proclaim and teach concerning the KINGDOM of God.

So the many years of trials, tribulations, testing, ups and downs, and gaining of revelation, I have been released to publish a book on the KINGDOM of God to urge the body of Christ to either shift to the KINGDOM PERSPECTIVE or make sure that everything thing they are doing is aligned to the KINGDOM of God.

The KINGDOM of God is such a vast topic because the ways and thoughts of the Most High King are infinite and his KINGDOM itself has no end. So, this book is more of an introduction at a high level of what has been revealed to me over the years concerning the great and everlasting KINGDOM of the Most High. With that said, this is the first book of a KINGDOM series with other books to come. Using a building analogy, this book is to serve as a foundation to be laid where other books will come to be the framework, wiring, plumbing, door and roof to bring more clarity as the KINGDOM series progresses.

I have been pregnant with this book for a decade. The book has been outlined for 3 years without any writing. Then the actual writing took 8 months due to breaks and spiritual warfare compared to my previous writings being completed in two to three months. So I am very excited about the publication of this book and very thankful that is completed. You know how in the bible we have the Gospels and they might be referred to as "The Gospel According To" Luke, John, Mark, or Matthew? This book will serve a manifesto that I consider to be the Gospel of the KINGDOM according to Dr. Martin Ellis Jr. as it has been revealed to me by the holy scriptures and by revelation of the Holy Spirit.

In this book, since the theme is all about the KINGDOM, you will see that every time you see the word "KINGDOM", it will be in full capitalization. Also, as you see scriptures, they are from the King James Version with very few exceptions. To bring emphasis on certain words within the scriptures shared, you will notice that some words are highlighted as they are in bold and underlined.

You might wonder why I am publishing this book when there seem to be so many other KINGDOM books out there. The answer is firstly, everyone as well as myself has a part in this KINGDOM mandate of our Heavenly Father. There is a people waiting on my voice so they can follow and there is a people waiting on your voice and actions so they can follow. The other reason is that less emphasis has been put on the KINGDOM of God in these modern times. The heart of the Father is very much about expanding his KINGDOM and this is the season where you will see him release strategically KINGDOM minded men and women of the Most High to sound the KINGDOM alarm to wake us up.

This book in conjunction with other books are here, if really accepted and understood, to change the trajectory of the body of Christ. There is a need for us as KINGDOM believers to change our perspective and began to see, enter, inherit, and enlarge the KINGDOM of God. There is a call for KINGDOM Sons to arise and manifest in the earth and he is wanting us to respond by pressing towards the mark of the prize of the high calling which is in Christ Jesus (Yeshua). It is my hope that you catch the vision of the KINGDOM PERSPECTIVE so that the KINGDOM of God can come alive in you to eventually operate through you. Be blessed KINGDOM people of the Most High!

Acknowledgement

I want to first acknowledge our Heavenly Father for entrusting me to write about something that is so dear to his heart. Also, thank you Holy Spirit and the spirit of revelation and wisdom for enlightening my eyes as you all are truly the writers of this book as I could not do this in my own strength.

I also, want to acknowledge my beautiful and anointed wife, LaRonda, who had to deal with me spending long evenings writing this book while not spending time with her. She helped with the editing and gave great suggestions for adjustments. Being the artsy and creative person she is, she provided guidance when it came to the front and back covers of the book. You gave your assistance even though you were very busy yourself with the plethora of things that you are involved in. Thanks you so much my Lovely for your help and for believing in me. You are loved and you are so appreciated.

I want to thank all others including my mother, Dr. Winnetta Ellis, who were responsible for my spiritual growth and who prayed for me to be an example of Christ in the earth and fulfill my KINGDOM ordained destiny.

Chapter 1: Introduction

From the dawn of time, there has always been a quest in man to conquer and occupy. A thirst to go where no one else has been and set up a new frontier has been in the heart of many. In the halls of history, there have been kings, queens, KINGDOMS, dynasties, and empires put in place for the purpose of leadership and in some cases domination. In some scenarios, these KINGDOMS were a blessing to humanity and in others, these KINGDOMS have not been the best examples of leadership and rule. There have been leaders who have held the people in their heart and have been led by that driving factor as their main motivation. On the other hand, some leaders because of fame, fortune and glory have made their own desires and agendas be their only concern. Because of the quest for domination, control, and territory, there have been many wars and casualties in the name of KINGDOM expansion and dominion. Sometimes in the context of KINGDOM conquest, it is not always a pretty picture of what happens behind the scene. This is the reality of KINGDOM dynamics we have seen in this world portrayed by men and women throughout the centuries.

*For t**he invisible things** of him **from the creation of the world are
clearly seen**, **being understood by the things that are made**, even
his eternal power and Godhead; so that they are without excuse:*
(Romans 1:20)

Based on the referenced scripture in Romans, I believe that the Most High allows things in the earth to be a picture and parallel to exemplify his spiritual concepts for the world to take notice. It is through an earthly example even if it is projected in an imperfect way that we can look at through certain lenses to catch an intended glimpse of that which is of the heavenly and perfect realm of the Most High. Our creator, the Most High, wants us to know him as a father. Therefore, he placed in the world the family dynamic so mankind can see up close what a father is. He wants us to know his Son as a husband in relation to the church. So in the garden, he places Adam and Eve to be one flesh. Through the family examples placed in the earth, it allowed a platform for the Most High to teach us about the type of relationships we should have with him and his Son Jesus (Yeshua), the Messiah.

In the same manner, He wants us to know the Father and Son as KING. It is his will and desire that we see the reality that there is an everlasting KINGDOM that is greater and bigger than anything we can imagine. In this KINGDOM, the Most High's goal is for us to look at good and bad examples of KINGDOMS that he allowed us to observe on the earth to discern what a KINGDOM is and what a KINGDOM is not. From taking that which is natural and translating it to that which is spiritual, he wants us to come into the conclusive knowledge that the great and unending KINGDOM of the Most High is superior and more glorious than anything we have laid our natural eyes on or even our mind can fathom. What we have seen as an earthly exhibition pales in comparison in terms of quantity and quality when compared to the true substance of His KINGDOM. And just think! He is giving us an invitation to this place that he lives in, moves, has His being, and calls his own.

What Is A KINGDOM?

Before moving along, let's discuss on some level about what a KINGDOM is. In simple words, a KINGDOM is a territory that is ruled by a king. The word "KINGDOM" is a compound of the words "king" and "dom" which is short for domain. There is no KINGDOM without a king and a domain (territory) being in place. A person can be a self proclaimed king but if there is no domain, then this person is not a king of a KINGDOM. This reminds me of some people in the church today who have self-appointed titles like "bishop" or "pastor" but have no flock or following to substantiate the title claim. There can be a community of people and a land that has calculated borders, but if there is not a government where there is a ruling person, then this is not a KINGDOM. A KINGDOM is a living organism and construct of a king, a people, a land, and a law of the land that has possibilities of expansion or destruction. A KINGDOM is a multi-faceted entity that has goals and strategy to increase in power without any intent of ever being overthrown.

A KINGDOM can have many layers, components, and dimensions to it. Below are listed some components of a powerful KINGDOM that will be referenced to at times in this book:

- **Domain** - the territory that the reign of the KINGDOM extends to
- **King** - the head and ruler over the KINGDOM territory that is assigned to them
- **Laws** - the system of rules which a KINGDOM recognizes as regulating the actions of its members and by which it may be enforced by the imposition of penalties
- **Government** - the governing body of the designated KINGDOM territory and domain along with its hierarchy where the King is the executive head of that government
- **Military** - the collective of branches of armed forces that is a heavily

armed, with weapons and tools, highly organized force primarily intended for warfare where each branch specializes in certain areas with strategy and rank

- **Agenda** - a vision, plan, strategy and possibly timeline of something to be completed or done by the KINGDOM
- **Protocol** – the official procedure or system of rules when it comes to engaging with governing entities and with warfare against enemies and with allies
- **Culture** - the customs, arts, social institutions, and achievements of the KINGDOM
- **Language** - a system of communication used by a particular region
- **Headquarters** - a place from which an KINGDOM and its military operation is controlled
- **Bloodline** - a set of ancestors or line of descent of a person that is considered royal
- **Inheritance** - the acquisition or possession of rule from past generations and through the line of succession

By looking at the natural and simple definition of what all consist of a KINGDOM, we can begin to see a picture and parallel of the workings of the KINGDOM of the Most High. The Heavenly Father is King of the everlasting KINGDOM to which there is no end. The complete realm in its totality of the heavens and earth is his territory that is ever expanding to populate and penetrate areas of darkness with the light of the KINGDOM. The angels of the Most High and mankind as His creation are the people of the KINGDOM that He is calling to a place of aligning to His KINGDOM purposes, decrees, and laws. There is a culture and language that is the core fabric and heartbeat of His KINGDOM. Also, there is a bloodline and inheritance that is made available to those who are born again of the blood of his Son. Once again, this is just a skeleton picture of the KINGDOM. But this picture in its simplicity is way more exciting than just thinking about living a life on earth, going to church, and maybe you might get a mansion one day in the sweet by and by.

I have defined what a KINGDOM is from a general point of view but when we are talking about the KINGDOM of God or KINGDOM of heaven, I have been given the following definition. The KINGDOM of the Most High is the rule and reign of the Most High and Christ **in you**, **above or over you**, and **through you** with the intention to be all in all. Of course, more elaboration of this definition will come later in this book.

Heaven Vs. The KINGDOM of God

Many aim in this journey of salvation is to one day when they breathe their last breath or either when the Messiah cracks the sky, that they can possibly go through those pearly gates of heaven where there is a mansion waiting for them as they enjoy a great time of joy, peace, and happiness. This is an interesting view but I will later argue in this book that it is a short-sighted and very limited perspective when it comes to the grand scheme of salvation and the reason for Christ dying on the cross for our sins. God is creator of the heavens (plural), the earth, many galaxies, and the list can go on. And this long list of God's creation and what is under his umbrella represents the KINGDOM of God.

There are different levels or layers to what is referred to as "the heavens". Some believe that there is a 3rd heaven where God dwells, a 2nd heaven where the battle of the angels and fallen angels take place, and the 1st heaven that represents the atmosphere of the earth. So with the "heaven" aim, one might ask which heaven are you going to? Is this the only portion allocated to us in the vast KINGDOM of God? But mankind is not just servants who are getting a piece of a pie type of reward at the end. We are so much more and have so much more at stake.

Mankind in God's eye is what he created to be in his image and likeness to rule over a given territory that is more-inclusive than just heaven. Christ came down from his glory to die on the cross for more than just our sins to be forgiven and for us to just die and go to heaven. He died so that his blood justifies us and gives us access to the throne of the KINGDOM to be joint heirs in the rulership of the KINGDOM of God. This notion comes more with implications that we are supposed to have an intimate relationship with the Father, come to a place of maturity and conformity to the image of the Son (Christ), and walk in a full responsibility of all things that are dominion related in the KINGDOM of God. To only aim for heaven minimizes the scope of what the Father had intended. When the bible says that blessed is he or she who is meek for they shall inherit the earth, then this does not align with a just going to heaven view.

Now Vs. Later

Now some might have the argument that they do believe in the KINGDOM of God but see it more as a dispensational mark that will come later at the end of the world when Christ returns to the earth. We will wait in heaven until that time and then we can be joint heirs with him and rule later when he establishes his KINGDOM on the earth. I hear you but this thinking places all KINGDOM rule and authority to the believer to be when Christ returns later down the road.

What about the commandment of our Lord and Christ in Matthew 6:33 that encourages the believer to seek "first" the KINGDOM of God and his righteousness? Why would we seek something FIRST that we can't have until later after we die? Why would we be told to seek and then we will find or to knock and the door will be open when it is in fact delayed and for us later? Then also you have in John 3 where Christ tells Nicodemus that he must be born again to see and enter the KINGDOM of God.

Christ also states that the KINGDOM of God is without observation and that it is not of this world. But he also lets us know because you don't see the KINGDOM of God or him in the physical realm and with your physical eyes, it does not mean it is not operating on the earth. That is why the Lord has admonished believers to pray that the KINGDOM come and that the will of heaven be manifested on the earth. We are told by scripture that we ARE a chosen generation, holy nation, and a royal priesthood right now. Apostle John in the book of Revelation points out in the first chapter that Christ made us kings and priests now. I can go on these lines for a while but these points will be elaborated on more later in the book. The key objective for this section is to make the reader begin to think of the possibility that there is a KINGDOM of God that we are to see and enter in NOW.

The Mark & The Prize

*I press toward **the mark** for **the prize** of the high calling of God in Christ Jesus. (Philippians 3:10)*

Going back to the time of John the Baptist, he came on the scene and began the proclamation of the KINGDOM of the Most High with the following words: "The KINGDOM is at hand". For John the Baptist to declare this, there must have been an expectation for a KINGDOM to manifest. Why else would it have been significant to him and his eventual followers for him to proclaim such a statement. Indeed, there was a focus of the people of the Most High, thousands of years ago, on the things of the KINGDOM of the Most High. Up until this time we are in right now, that focus has been watered down and deflected.

Today, the focus in most of the body of Christ is church buildings, programs, and a weak hyper grace message of just believing in Christ the Messiah so converts can go to heaven. The bar of what to strive and reach for has been lowered and our mindset has shifted to scramble our priorities in this faith journey. We are to press towards the mark for the prize of the high calling which is in Christ the Messiah. Here are some questions that come to mind when I read the preceding sentence. What mark are we pressing towards? What is the prize? What is the high calling? What does it mean by the prize being "in" Christ the Messiah? In short, all these answers revolve around "THE KINGDOM of the MOST HIGH".

Many come to Christ because they are scared to go to hell. Some come because they just want to go to heaven. Some come to Christ because it seems to be the thing to do because they saw relatives and friends do the same and they just followed suit. A lot of this stems from how the message is being packaged to the world and in the churches. The central theme in the message should always be THE KINGDOM and the new covenant that the Most High has initiated to the world through Christ.

It is like a salesman who is selling a product that has ten features but only tells them about two features of the product. Even though the customer bought the product, they never utilized the product to its full potential. The customer also might have just opened the box of the product and began to use it without first even reading the owner's manual to view its full capabilities. How surprised and maybe disappointed will the owner be if they found out what they possessed all this time had so much more functionality and value. This is what we are seeing that some of us are not pressing to their full potential because it is misunderstood what the true mark and target is.

The result of not having all the aspects of the gospel of the KINGDOM being proclaimed causes a paradigm of people who are coming to the KINGDOM because of fear, ignorance (lack of full understanding), and selfish intentions. The results are that more converts that have a scaled down version of Christianity are being created instead of disciples of Christ that understand the goal and purpose of the KINGDOM of God. But the KINGDOM of God is a KINGDOM of selfless love, relationship, knowledge, and surrender to the will of the KING. Instead of wanting what we want and having our own agenda, we need to align to want what the KING wants. My prayer is that through this book, that we will come to know the true intention of the Most High and the true potential of the believer concerning the KINGDOM of God. May we come to the place that every action, thought, and intent shift to the point of view of THE KINGDOM PERSPECTIVE.

Chapter 2 : The KINGDOM Agenda

In today's society we hear a lot about the gospel of the Messiah. Its emphasis is usually on things like his death, burial, and resurrection and if you only believe then when you die you can go to heaven. So mostly a lot of time while people are out recruiting or "witnessing" for souls, the word "KINGDOM" rarely comes up. And this is a travesty because besides the Most High's name and his ways, he wants you to think about his promise of the "KINGDOM". He wants you to look at things from the KINGDOM perspective and the KINGDOM lens. This shift in view and thinking will begin to open up other revelations on what the Most High is revealing in his Word. The main goal and reward is not for you to die and go to heaven, but what the goal and the pearl of great price is, is actually the KINGDOM of the Most High. He wants you to be in position to see, enter, and inherit the KINGDOM. From the bible, we can see that God's agenda and intention has always been about the KINGDOM.

KINGDOM Mandate In the Garden

The emphasis and theme of the "KINGDOM" has always been in the heart of the Father. When we ponder on what happened in the garden of Eden during creation in the first few chapters of Genesis, it is obvious that KINGDOM was in his mind. The word "KINGDOM" is broken up from two words to mean the king's domain. The Most High is the KING of all the universe and creation and he was creating a domain for him to rule and reign over. His domain of his KINGDOM is the heavens and the earth. His intention was not to rule by himself but to create out of all creation a royal bloodline who will reign with him. That is why he said (Gen. 1:26) "Let us create man in our own image and likeness". What is that image? It is an image of a righteous, loving, creative, powerful King. And when we are thinking of likeness, that speaks to spiritual DNA. I have children and because I passed my DNA to them, they have taken on some of my "likeness". He is building here in the earth a royal family that has his attributes and likeness for the sake of a KINGDOM dynasty.

> *27 So **GOD created man in his own image**, in the image of GOD*
> *created he him; male and female created he them. **28** And GOD*
> ***blessed them**, and GOD said unto them, **Be fruitful, and multiply,***
> ***and replenish the earth, and subdue it: and have dominion over***
> *the fish of the sea, and over the fowl of the air, and over every living*
> *thing that moveth upon the earth.(Genesis 1:27-28)*

So we have talked about the bloodline that the Most High was creating to operate in KINGDOM function. But we have not talked about the KINGDOM mandate that he gave Adam and Eve during creation. As we can see from the above scriptures that the Most High (Father) gave a commandment using terms like "fruitful", "multiply", replenish", "the earth", "dominion over". These words are powerful words that indicate his KINGDOM intentions. To be fruitful and multiply implies to enlarge your territory and your bloodline. It implies to plant roots and seeds and watch it be fruitful. It speaks to destiny and purpose. Then we have the phrase of "replenish the earth" which speaks to the "earth" not "heaven" per se being your domain. That is why we see scriptures like "Blessed is the meek for they shall inherit the earth". For there to be a KINGDOM, there has to be a domain. And lastly, we see in the above Genesis verse, the words "dominion over". The Father's intention for Adam and Eve who was made in his image, likeness, and DNA was for them to have KINGDOM dominion. The Father's intention from the beginning was THE KINGDOM.

Image First

*And God said, Let us make man in **our image**, after **our likeness**: and let them have **dominion** over the fish of **the sea**, and over the fowl of **the air,** and over the cattle, and over all **the earth**, and over every creeping thing that creepeth upon the earth. (Genesis 1:26)*

In Genesis 1:26, it is evident that the Most High's intention is for there to be a type of people created who bears an image and likeness that enables them to have the capacity to rule and have dominion in three domains: the sea, the air, and the earth. So the domain of this KINGDOM of God is greater than the earth but also includes other domains as well. But the key is that there is only one type of person who can rule in these domains. It has to be one who is made in a particular image and likeness. It is what some like to refer to as the "God-kind". I am not saying that we are God or the Most High but we are of his species that is made in his image and his likeness.

I want to draw your attention that this image and likeness that was given to man did not refer to a being saying make man in "my image and likeness" but it says "our image" and "our likeness". This implies that there were multiple persons bearing "one" image in the time of this creation. It also shows the Most High was in the business of multiplying himself in a way where many will bear his image and likeness. That before man, the Most High already had the Son and the Holy Spirit bearing his image and likeness. There is one image and likeness that matters in the eyes of the Most High. That is why the Messiah while on the earth says "when you see me, you have seen the Father" because he was bearing his image and likeness. Even though they were different personalities with their own will, they were "one" because they had the same image and likeness.

The way that the Most High orchestrated it was that "image" only can rule and be partakers of his KINGDOM. I hear a lot of people say "we are God's image". Even those who have not given their lives to Christ at all. If a person is not living for Christ, then that declaration is untrue. The reason for this assertion was that Adam when originally made was made in the image of the Godhead but after the fall, he lost that image and likeness and no longer was able to rule and have dominion in the way the Most High intended. He lost his glory, his authority, and his position in the KINGDOM of GOD. And not only he lost it but every offspring after him that carried his seed and DNA had a tainted image as well. Hence, the need for a savior.

The Messiah (Jesus / Yeshua) declared that for us to enter the KINGDOM of GOD, we must be born again. Why did we need to be born again? The reason is because we no longer carried the image and likeness of God and we needed to be born again by the Spirit of God to not only see the KINGDOM but to also enter the KINGDOM. By repentance and by faith accepting the sacrifice of Christ, we put ourselves in a position to be born again and bear a new image so we can be a new creation within a new covenant. There is no way we can truly reign in the KINGDOM of GOD without the image and likeness being reinstated to us. The KINGDOM is for a specific bloodline that looks like our Heavenly Father.

*For whom he did foreknow, he also did predestinate to be **conformed to the image of his Son**, that he might be the firstborn among many brethren. (Romans 8:29)*

As the previous scripture shows, the Most High had a destiny in mind for us before the foundation of the world. And the call that we were predestined for was to be conformed and made into the "image" of the Son. This is all of mankind's first call; to be a mature Son in his KINGDOM. Literally the goal is to look and be like the Son so we can be joint heirs among the firstborn Son. This is why Christ is able to say you are joint-heirs with me because as we are born again, we carry the "image". And it is the "image" that has a right to rule, have dominion, and their rightful seat in the KINGDOM of GOD.

Image - Likeness - KINGDOM

Some might think of image and likeness as the same thing. But it is not. Image speaks to a reflection that is connected to an original source that projects itself in a different location or direction. The image is not the source but an expression of the source so much that by looking at the image you have an idea what the source looks like. In Hebrews 1, it states that Christ is the "express image" of the Father. The Father and Son are one in terms of image but have their own mind and will. That is why Christ says, "not my will but thy will". Or he says that he came to do the will of the Father. Even though the Son is the image, he still has to submit himself and will to be LIKE the Father (likeness).

Image is what spiritual beings see of a person in the spiritual realm. In other words, God the Father is a spirit and his image is spiritual. Mankind is a tripartite being that is spirit, soul, body. So the image deals with the spirit of man, where the likeness deals with the soul and body. I want to say it this way. The image is who you are in terms of DNA but likeness deals with your nature, character, and how you act and behave. A man can father a child and through DNA that son when it grows up has a similar image of that father. But to be LIKE the Father, that son has to have certain actions, choices, and even mannerisms, for someone to say that son acts LIKE their father.

The Most High has a progression. When we receive Christ in our lives, our spirit man (image) is renewed instantly. But the likeness of us in the aspect of our heart, soul, body, and actions takes some time to mature in. Someone can be born again and carry the image and be an infant in terms of likeness in respect to being "like" God. A father can have a son and we can see a resemblance (image) but it is not until that son grows up into a place of maturity where we can say he not only looks like him (image) but also acts like him (likeness). The progression is to have a renewed spirit (image) that leads to a renewed heart, mind, soul, and body (likeness). When we bear a new image like Christ and begin to let the working of the Holy Spirit invade our other areas, then we can become like Him and begin to truly rule in the KINGDOM of God. The true sign of a Son of the KINGDOM is to do only what we see the Father doing; truly being the image and the likeness of the Most High in all the domains he has given to us.

The KINGDOM Agenda Now

And the seventh angel sounded; and there were great voices in heaven, saying, The KINGDOMS of this world are become the KINGDOMS of our Lord, and of his Christ; and he shall reign for ever and ever.
(Revelation 11:15)

The KINGDOM is for Christ, which is the image that reigns from the highest heaven. Christ is a many-membered body (1 Cor. 12:12-20) and the Messiah is the head of the body and we are the rest of the body. Our first call is to be conformed to the image and likeness that comes along with the authority to rule. It is the destiny of the KINGDOM of God to take over the KINGDOMS of this world and for Christ (Messiah the Head and his joint heirs) to possess the KINGDOM.

Some are thinking this is when you die and be in the sweet by and by but the KINGDOM is for NOW. The KINGDOM is to be sought for NOW. It is NOW that the Most High wants to restore the earth back to Eden and even beyond. It is his desire NOW to turn parts of the KINGDOM in darkness into the KINGDOM of light. The Most High has proclaimed that he is doing a new thing, bringing his people into a new covenant with his goal for there to be a new heaven and new earth. The whole creation is waiting for the manifestation of the Sons of God who bear the image of Christ. The Most High's agenda is to reign over it all and have his KINGDOM offspring be in dominion with him in every facet and territory of the KINGDOM of God. We must press to live in this NOW KINGDOM perspective.

Chapter 3 : The KINGDOM Territories

The KINGDOM of Heaven

In the introduction of this book, certain components of the KINGDOM were listed and here I want to emphasize that there is a King of the KINGDOM which is Christ our Lord who is King of Kings and Lord of Lords. We as Sons of the KINGDOM are the kings and lords under the King of Kings and Lord of Lords. Once the image and likeness is established in us as believers then we can exercise our dominion as Sons in the different areas of the KINGDOM such as the highest heavens, the air, the sea, the earth, and the realm of fire (hell). These are the domains of the KINGDOM of GOD.

The flow of the KINGDOM of God is from heaven to earth. There is a principle in the Spirit that says that which is higher rules over that which is lower. That is why we call our Heavenly Father the "Most High" because there is none higher than him . He is the Highest of the High. Lucifer in

Isaiah 14:13 understanding this principle declared within himself that he will ascend into heaven and exalt his throne "above" the stars of God.

Lucifer saw that for him to be the top person in the KINGDOM that he had to go into heaven and exalt himself higher than stars. Lucifer first of all had a throne but his throne was not in the highest heaven and not higher than the atmosphere of the stars. In his heart, he wanted to be greater (not even like) than the Most High and to do that he tried with his gathered army of fallen angels attempted to overtake the throne of the Most High. He wanted to be the top king of the KINGDOM of Heaven. But the Most High wasn't having none of that. Hence, the fall of Lucifer.

But this shows that there is a realm that is the highest in the KINGDOM of God and that is the KINGDOM of Heaven. The KINGDOM of Heaven and The KINGDOM of God are the same KINGDOM but from a different perspective. We know these are the same because the Gospels have the same scriptures and use the "KINGDOM of God" and the "KINGDOM of Heaven" interchangeably. The KINGDOM of God points to whose KINGDOM it is. That is why we say at the end of the Lord's prayer, "thine is the KINGDOM, the power, and the glory forever". The word "thine" points to ownership or the highest authority. Whereas the KINGDOM of Heaven speaks of the highest realm of the KINGDOM from which the government of the KINGDOM flows into the lower dimensions of earth. Alluding to the Lord's prayer once again, we see the heart of the Lord's prayer is "thy KINGDOM come, thy will be done on earth as it is in heaven". The Most High wants his KINGDOM to reign and rule from the realm of the highest heaven and trickle down to the lowest realms of the KINGDOM so that earth may look just like heaven.

The KINGDOM of the Air

In Genesis 1, the Most High wanted mankind to have dominion over the "fowls of the air". Someone might read that and feel he is talking about birds like ravens, pigeons, eagles and the such. But I believe the Most High who is a spirit and who sees everything from a spiritual perspective is talking about more than what we see in the physical realm as birds. He is referring to a realm of the air that has spiritual entities and creatures in it. He is referring to the atmosphere that has a spiritual real estate that includes thrones, mountains, stars, the sun, the moon, and the list goes on. And it was the Most High's design for mankind to rule in this domain of the air.

To have dominion over a particular area or type of creature, you need to have the ability to enter into that area, realm, or dimension and also be able to do what the inhabitants of that space are able to do and then some. I know I sound like I am going off the deep end a bit. But Adam and Eve in the fall, lost access to certain spaces and places and lost their authority and their ability to do what they could do before the fall. But as Sons of the KINGDOM of God, Christ came to reinstate us to have access to all provincial arenas of the KINGDOM and be able to sit with him in heavenly places.

These powers of the dimensions of the air were delivered to satan (Luke 4:6) by Adam when Adam fell. If he fell, that implies that Adam and the state of a man fell from one higher plane of existence to a lower plane of existence where instead of knowing the realms of the spirit and air, they only knew the earth from a physical perspective. This is why satan is known as the "prince of power of the air" (Ephesians 2:2). He is not the prince of the air but of the prince of the "power" of the air. The true kings and heirs of the air are us as the believers of Christ. We are the kings of the realm of the air but he is the "prince" not "king" to the power of the air. This is because most of us don't understand our authority and position in the heavenlies which allows satan to still operate with the power and influence of the air.

Ephesians 2:2 also shows that the person who is using the power of the air also is able to control those who are ignorant of their position and authority and cause them to walk according to the course of this world. That which operates in the lower realm will be controlled by that which operates in a higher realm. We need not to be ignorant of satan's devices or who we are as born again believers so we can rule with Christ sitting together with him in heavenly places.

For we wrestle not against flesh and blood, but against principalities, against powers, against the rulers of the darkness of this world, against **spiritual wickedness in high places.** *(Ephesians 6:12)*

We are battling against entities like principalities and powers that cultivate spiritual wickedness in high places (the air). There is a lot of talk about the constellations and star signs (the zodiac). Someone might proclaim, " I am a Gemini". Another might say, "I am a Taurus". When such proclamations are made, that person is agreeing that they were born in the flesh under a certain configuration of the sun, moon, and stars and therefore, will act according to a group of rules that the atmosphere is dictating for them to behave. You might have been born in the flesh as a Scorpio or Leo but once you are born again you are no longer under the obligation to do what the sun, moon, and stars say. But, now you are under the sign, seal, and covering of Christ and he is your King for you to obey him. Now you sit with him higher in a place that is above all principalities, power, sun, moon, and stars.

This realm of the Air is the realm where certain witches and warlocks operate in the night hours as they astral project and have strategy meetings to wreak havoc through the earth. The bible refers to the "Queen of Heaven" all throughout the book of Jeremiah because there are principalities that are on the side of darkness that are working with human agents to control things in the affairs of nations and people in the earth. I remember a quote that went something like, those who own the wealth have the power to write what is in the history books. I want to point this notion to the spiritual realm that those who occupy the realms of the KINGDOM of the air will have power to impact the earth. KINGDOM Sons and believers, we must learn how to operate and take our place in the KINGDOM of the air so we can bring heaven to earth.

The KINGDOM of the Water

There is so much more that can be said about the KINGDOM of the air but let's look at the KINGDOM of the Water. I am a firm believer that things like television shows and movies, even though they might be categorized as fantasy, are actually giving you glimpses into hidden things of the spiritual world. When I was younger, there was a Disney movie by the name of Little Mermaid and now in the 2020s a remake has come forth of this movie. This movie features a sea princess that originated from an underwater KINGDOM. We live in a time where you have the DC character of Aquaman and if you study the legend or lore of that character, you see he came from a marine civilization that had their own technology, government, and royal hierarchy.

The second Black Panther movie of Marvel Comics featured a nemesis to the KINGDOM of Wakanda who was basically king and leader of a marine civilization. And lastly, I want to point our attention to the second Avatar movie where the first movie featured people of the land but now the sequel featured people of the water. There are so many more references we can pull from TV shows and movies that are hinting to an underwater community. The entertainment industry and media are definitely dropping hints to intrigue us and prepare us who are not paying attention to be vulnerable to these realms.

Even from ancient times, there have been legends and references from mythology that point to water civilizations. In the Scotland area, you have the legend of the Loch Ness monster which is this gigantic creature that lives and rules in the water. Many are on record of seeing mermaids in lakes, rivers, seas, and oceans. Homer in *Iliad* and *Odyssey* mentions the sirens of the sea that through their songs can hypnotize men to cause them to shipwreck. It is not all fantasy but points to some aspect of reality and truth. Even the bible has four references to the creature "leviathan" that is a serpent being that lives in the water.

There are quite a number of references from books, television, movies, personal testimonies, historical accounts, and even the bible that keep this discussion going. I want to submit to you that there is a marine KINGDOM where depending on the area of the world you point to, you have the Queen of the Coast and the Queen of the Sea who are in charge. There is a hierarchy that occurs in these places of water and best believe through their government and rule they are trying to carry out an agenda.

Some men and women in the earth have made covenants with the marine world to be their agents in the earth. Even preachers and false prophets are making deals with these entities so they can flow in supernatural power. None of this is for free so of course, they require blood and sacrifice and also participation in certain sexual rituals.

The reach of the marine KINGDOM is vast in that they are even impacting and infiltrating people's dreams. The effects of this range from sexual perversion, diseases, infertility, curses, problems with relationships and so many other things. Some are so yoked to those of the marine KINGDOM that these spiritual spirits claim humans as their spouses. Some are plagued by jealous spiritual husbands and spiritual wives that meet them in their dreams. And even worse, some are being raped by these entities in the night hours while they are sleep.

This marine world has cities and even laboratories where new technology is being created so they can manipulate mankind. A lot of things like beauty products are created in the sea world that contain spiritual substances from the marine world so it can impart curses and damages. A lot of these products pay homage to the Queen of the Sea by their name or logo. For example, you have Starbucks coffee company who has the marine Queen in the logo. They are creating dances and types of music down there and a lot of the entertainment like music artists have contracts with the marine world. We have to be careful what we do, eat, listen to, wear and even what trends we follow and mimic because it is all spiritual and has a source from somewhere.

All these areas that are aspects of the KINGDOM can be their own book but my focus is just to mention to bring awareness. It is the Most High's intention for us not to be ruled by these entities but for us to rule over them. It is interesting that in John 3, the Messiah tells Nicodemus that we need to be born again of the water to enter the KINGDOM of God. Also, in heaven you have the river of life. Originally the waters were separated from being all together into the waters above and the waters below. Once again, the waters below must be like the waters above. So much in the bible alludes that water is special to God: rivers of living water, fountain of life, water baptism, and etc. This is another area as seen in Genesis that Adam and his descendants are supposed to rule. Thank the Most High that his Son has repaired the breach to bring us back into the place of KINGDOM authority.

The KINGDOM of the Earth

When it comes to the KINGDOM of the earth as I alluded to earlier, it is a mixture of the networks of the KINGDOMS of this world. When Christ went into the wilderness and was visited by the enemy during his temptation, satan took him to a pinnacle and offered to him that these are the KINGDOMS of the world that were "delivered" to him. Adam was created to rule these KINGDOMS of the world but through the fall satan became "god" (lowercase g) of this world.

Note that there is a difference between the earth and the world. They come from different Hebrew and Greek words in the bible. Earth might be linked to the word we see as "cosmos" where the world is linked to the word "age". The Most High owns the earth and all that is within it. The Christ per Daniel 7 possesses the KINGDOMS of this world but satan to those who are not in the know operates as the "god" of this world. The earth is the real estate and domain but the world is the age, system, and illusion that is running on top of the real estate. It is like the earth is the hardware and the world is the software app or operating system running on top of the hardware.

But there is one hardware but the enemy has his version of operating system and the Most High has his version. We live in a world where most people know that in the computer world, the majority of computers are PC compatible or an Apple (Mac) computer. Usually the PC compatible machine will run the operating system of Windows while an Apple (Mac) machine will run a version of a MacOS operating system. And on the earth, the problem is that you have hardware like "the earth" that was supposed to run with the operating system of "KINGDOM of God" but the enemy got his operating system of "KINGDOM in darkness" running on it.

And just like Apple and Windows don't play nice with each other, when the KINGDOM in darkness is trying to operate in the earth that the Most High created for the KINGDOM of God, then there is the problem. So the Most High had to send Christ to come and do a factory reset, so he can install the KINGDOM of God operating system. Then we create apps with the code of the master programmer (Christ) that are supposed to run on the hardware of the earth. Sorry, I have an IT background so this analogy is what came to mind by the Holy Spirit.

Just like the air and water, there is a government that exists. We see the obvious that is visible to us. From a United States perspective, we see that nations have presidents, states have governors, and cities have mayors. There are aldermen and council members in other areas. But there is a spiritual side behind these visible posts that most people are not considering. And as the KINGDOM of God is invading the earth there is a battle between the body of Christ and the agents of the enemy for who controls what.

In the KINGDOM of the air, there are fallen angels and principalities that operate there. But on the earth demons operate and can even possess human beings. There are witches, warlocks, and sorcerers that are influenced by and have relationships with demons. These agents of satan use witchcraft and spells to manipulate things on the earth. Witches and warlocks use things from the earth realm to concoct their potions and do their spells upon their evil altars. Things like herbs, dirt, trees, minerals, crystals, rocks, metal and the such are utilized to wreak havoc in the earth. Of course there are witches who claim they are good witches and not evil witches and that there are two categories. But the key factor is they are not part of the KINGDOM of God because if you are not aligning to the will of the KING and you are using some other source of power for the sake of your own will and agenda, then you all are on the dark side.

The fight between the light of the KINGDOM of God and the KINGDOM in darkness on the earth is for the different realms of influences. Some might have heard of the seven mountains of influence which became popular through Christian leaders, Loren Cunningham and Dr. Bill Bright in the 1970s. This model asserts that there are seven mountains or realms of influence that we must invade as believers to make an impact in the earth. These seven mountains are : Religion, Family, Education, Government, Media, Arts & Entertainment, and Business. Even though you don't see the exact mountains in the bible, I believe these areas do paint a landscape of some of the sub-territories of the earth that the enemy is trying to rule in. But the Most High is calling a royal and holy people who will make it their mandate to bring heaven to earth and manifest the KINGDOM of God everywhere and everyday of their lives..

The Territory of Fire (Hell and Death)

And God said, Let us make man in our image, after our likeness: and let them have dominion over the fish of the sea, and over the fowl of the air, and over the cattle, and over all the earth, and over every creeping thing that creepeth upon the earth. (Genesis 1:26)

Looking at Genesis 1:26, as stated before, we see the Most High's intention for man to rule in the air, the sea (water), and the earth. There is no implication to the territory of fire. This is because before the fall of Adam, the territory of fire was not a place to be ruled in. The intention of the territory of fire came into play when satan and the other fallen angels rebelled against the Most High. This was a place of imprisonment for some of them. (For there were different instances of rebellion but that is another conversation.) And after the fall of Adam, then it became a place of judgment for lost souls. This also became a place of satan where he utilized as a headquarters where he revels in the fact that some souls did not repent and now he can watch them have their place in hell, the territory of fire.

But Christ, in the mindset of the KINGDOM of God advancing and with the intention to one day take over all, when he died on the cross , he descended in hell and took the keys of death and hell as Revelation 1:18 proclaims. Christ's believers should be diligent to not let the gates of hell prevail and use the keys that Christ took to avoid the grips of hell and eternal death. The territory of fire was not the original plan and so the mandate was not to rule in it but operate in authority in realms and dimensions far above it.

The Enemy: The Counterfeiter

So we have talked about water and the air (wind). Also we have earth and fire as well. You might have noticed I just made the reference to what are called the four elements. And this might have made some of you nervous if you are not already nervous. I want to take the time to tell you that the enemy is a counterfeiter. He is not a creator of anything. He has to use things that were already created. The mysteries and hidden and secret knowledge are things that were taught to him.

So if the mention of the four elements strikes a nerve, then I encourage you to read the book of Genesis and the rest of the bible because the Most High are using them all over the place. In Hebrews, he is a consuming fire. In Revelation, the river or sea of living water proceeds from under the throne of the Most High. In Psalms, the earth is the Lord's and the fullness thereof. In Genesis, the Most High created the heavens and the earth. In John 3, the spirit of the Most High is related to the wind (air). The word spirit means "breath or air". In Acts, the Holy Spirit came like a mighty rushing wind (air). It is all in there. It is the KINGDOM believers' job to take back everything the enemy has stolen to gain for the sake of Christ.

KINGDOM Provinces for the KINGDOM of God

Many might look around and feel that the enemy is winning. It might look like the enemy has dominance in all these provinces and territories. The KINGDOM of God is without observation which means all the moves of the Most High are not visible or discerned by the natural man. The natural man can't see angels, demons, different realms and dimensions. The natural man does understand spiritual principles on how to manifest the KINGDOM of God in the earth. And in this lies the issue. The lost are not representing the KINGDOM of God in the earth and the majority of believers are not utilizing the keys of the KINGDOM to open the window of heaven to let it flow to earth. They work together and there is much overlap.

In this chapter, I have broken up things into the different KINGDOM provinces and territories to bring emphasis to the different parts but in reality there is much overlap between these territories. They are pieces to make one puzzle of the whole. One does not exist as a stand alone. The enemy and his network (KINGDOM in darkness) operates across all these territories and the dream and aim of the Most High is for his saints to rise up in revelation, power, and light and translate the KINGDOMS of darkness into KINGDOMS of marvelous light.

> *26 But the judgment shall sit, and they shall take away his dominion, to consume and to destroy it unto the end. 27 And the KINGDOM and dominion, and* **the greatness of the KINGDOM under the whole heaven, shall be given to the people of the saints of the most High,** *whose KINGDOM is an everlasting KINGDOM, and all dominions shall serve and obey him. (Daniel 7:26-27)*

The Most High have given the saints the power to possess the KINGDOM. The Most High wants it all and wants to redeem it all. His KINGDOM is an everlasting KINGDOM and it will not stop advancing until every domain and dominion serves and obeys him. Instead of us messing around with the marine KINGDOM, he wants us and the earth to be filled with the rivers of living water. Instead of mankind being captured by hell's fire, he wants a people who are purged by and baptized in the fire of the Most High. He is expecting his chosen and elect to realize they are already sitting together with him in heavenly places and displace the prince of the power of the air. Also, with the expectation of the kings and priests of the Most High, who we are, it is his desire for us to rise up and release the decrees of heaven into the earth to make all things new. The Most High wants it all.

Chapter 4 : The War For The Territory

In the previous chapter, outlined was that there are KINGDOM provincial territories and domains that the King's (Christ the Messiah) intention is to rule and reign over these areas. Even though, on Calvary so many years ago, Christ defeated the enemy with the cross and the resurrection, some aspects of Christ's KINGDOM are not realized yet. The reasons for this are numerous. One reason is that Christ, the head, has defeated the enemy but his body, us as believers, must do our part and overcome the enemy as well. Another reason is that the core of the KINGDOM of God is one that is spiritual, invisible on some level, and without observation to the natural eye. So the KINGDOM must be proclaimed, expanded, manifested and taken by force. KINGDOM domination is indeed a process of transferring that which is heavenly to the earth, that which is invisible to the visible (natural) realm, and that which is light to the areas of darkness. This process takes intention and time.

To bring this more to light and understanding, I want to use an example of the history of my ancestors. Being a Black American, my ancestors were enslaved and had certain rights and liberty taken from them. For them to be free from the slavery, a number of things had to happen. There was the Civil War and then in 1863, Abraham Lincoln released the Emancipation Proclamation to release the slaves which ended the "Civil War". (I am using this analogy at a very high level). Just because the Proclamation was established did not mean that everyone heard it right away. It did not mean every slave owner ended slavery right that second. It also did not mean every slave at that moment was freed from their actual situation. It took time from the time that Proclamation was signed , for messengers to get the word out and it took some physical en**force**ment to get the slave owners to align with the new way of doing things.

The Proclamation happened in 1863 but it was not until June 1865 where the last slaves were actually free. This is why my people celebrate Juneteenth as their true independence day. America was established as a nation in 1776 as a nation independent of Great Britain but there were still people enslaved. Even after freedom of physical slavery, there were levels of mental, emotional, financial, economic slavery that are still being fought against to bring liberty to us even to this day. After the "Civil War", the full war is still at play as we had to deal with Jim Crow laws, the fight for civil rights, police brutality, discrimination, and so much more. I outlined this so it will be obvious that real progress comes in layers and phases.

I was not trying to give a history lesson or stand on some type of soapbox, but my intention is to show that the KINGDOM of God is similar. The Heavenly Father had a plan and purpose for this world in the realm of eternity before the foundation of the world but after six days of creation he rested and knew that his plan had to play out in phases, dispensations, and through different covenants. Staying with the slavery analogy, Christ when he was on the earth made a proclamation of good news that the KINGDOM of God is at hand and he finished that proclamation on the cross when he said "It is finished". My point is that the Father in creation and Christ the Son who only does what he sees the Father does understand that he had to rest in his proclamation and watch it come to fruition over time in phases. I am telling you good people who are reading this book, that the KINGDOM of God is not an overnight thing. It is not an automatic thing given to us. The body of believers must align with the head and begin to walk out the victory that Christ the King has proclaimed. He is looking for ambassadors of the KINGDOM to go into all the world and proclaim the KINGDOM and get the word out. He is looking for warriors who will fight the good fight of faith to take territories for the KINGDOM because we have an enemy who is against the new regime and covenant and he wants to block, stop, and slow down the KINGDOM expansion. In simple terms, we are in a war and KINGDOM expansion can't happen without war.

We Are At War

*And from the days of John the Baptist until now the **KINGDOM** of heaven suffereth **violence**, and the violent **take it by force**. (Matthew 11:12)*

The KINGDOM of God is more than just hearing about Christ, then joining a social club like church filled with gimmicks and programs where you hear motivational speaking encouraging you to do "good works" so that when you die, you go to heaven. The KINGDOM of God is a KINGDOM that requires sacrifice, intention and violence. The KINGDOM of God, if not handled correctly, can be life or death. This is the seriousness of the KINGDOM of God. Matthew 11:12 shows us that the KINGDOM of heaven works with violence and the violent have to take it by force. The words "violence"and "force" implies that warfare goes hand in hand with the KINGDOM of God.

The KINGDOM of God is not for the faint of heart. I know we are at a time where the gospel message makes everything seem like lily pads, candy, beds of roses and rainbows. But we have a real enemy and we are standing many times on a battlefield. Violence is not pretty. It can be messy and at times bloody as we see with Christ on the cross. As I like to say at times, "The KINGDOM comes with violence. We are at war and war is violent and can come with casualties".

In the natural world, war in most cases occurs because someone or governments are trying to expand their KINGDOM territory and influence. Some are trying to build empires. They are using military means with weapons where death and devastation is a by-product of war. Some if they are not put to death become prisoners or hostages of war. There are times when to be on the offense and when to be on the defense. That which applies to the natural world, also applies to the KINGDOM of God.

*Confirming the souls of the disciples, and exhorting them to continue in the faith, and that we must through **much tribulation** enter **into the KINGDOM of God**. (Acts 14:22)*

We must enter the KINGDOM of God through war and "much" tribulation. The parable of the sower lets us know that once the seed of the KINGDOM is sown, the enemy is coming for it immediately to uproot it. I am here to let you know to be sober, vigilant, arise, and fight to see, enter, and inherit the KINGDOM. You have to fight to see the KINGDOM of God increase and be enlarged in your life and throughout the world. One word I have said a number of times in this book is the word "intention". You must be intentional when it comes to the KINGDOM of God. You must have to have an assertive and aggressive mindset to overcome the enemy and take the KINGDOM of God by force. We as believers must see the reality of this war. And once we see this reality, then we can understand the urgency of the KINGDOM because there can be lasting effects of war. Every move you make has major consequences. This war is not one battle but a series of battles. It is a long ball game and process that takes endurance. The race is not given to the swift but to the one who endures to the end. The athlete who wants the crown must "strive" for the mastery of their sport to be champion. We must press into the KINGDOM with a warfare mindset and fight the good fight of the KINGDOM.

The Battle for Territories and Domains

Once we come to grips that we are at war, then we have to grasp what we are fighting for and also how to obtain that which we are fighting for. Going back to the definition of a KINGDOM, it is the domain of the King. A domain is the totality of the realm of the King's rule that he has occupied and has dominion over. Within that KINGDOM domain, there can be territories or regions that make up the KINGDOM. These territories can be seen as slices of the KINGDOM pie. One intention of the KINGDOM of God is to continually expand and increase. The KINGDOM domain is increased by the adding of territories. In the war of the KINGDOM, the defense is to maintain the KINGDOM rule of the already obtained territories. The offense is to obtain more territories. The battles of the war are held at territorial markers (strongholds) to gain or to defend a particular area of the KINGDOM domain.

Battles can be won but know that the war continues. The war continues because firstly, there is more to gain but secondly, also there is an enemy who if we are not careful will try to re-occupy old territories. We see this in the parable of the sower where it was explained that the enemy comes immediately but if he does not uproot the word right away, he will try things later in the process to destroy the seed and its harvest (Matthew 13). Also, in Luke 4 when Christ was tempted by the enemy and won, scriptures let us know that the enemy left only to regroup and come back at a more opportune time. Another example in Matthew 12:43-35, we see that when an unclean spirit comes out of a man, he wanders and then eventually comes back to see if the house is still empty. The enemy does not stop and just like some of the old slave owners of old in the slavery analogy, he wishes that things can go back to the way it used to be.

You as the reader might wonder which provincial territories need to be gained and maintained. The answer is that it is mostly the same territories mentioned in the preceding chapter which are as follows:

- Inner KINGDOM
- First Heaven (physical)
- Second heaven (spiritual)
- Third Heaven (Highest of Heavens)
- The earth
- Realm of hell
- The sea

Without repeating myself, I will touch on these territories very quickly. I started with the Inner KINGDOM because we need the image to rule and reign.

The Inner KINGDOM comprises the heart (imagination and intentions), mind (thoughts), soul (emotions and will), and tongue (words). If this territory is not taken first by Christ, it is not much more we can do when it comes to the KINGDOM. The KINGDOM of God starts within us. There is a whole chapter later on this.

The KINGDOM of God flows in the direction from heaven to earth. So that which is above impacts that which is below. So the KINGDOM of Heaven through KINGDOM ambassadors who have the Inner KINGDOM (Christ) within them is released on the earth. The KINGDOM of Heaven is the combination of the Highest of Heavens or Third Heaven, the Second Heaven, and the First Heaven. The Highest of Heavens is where the Father dwells and his throne and temple resides. The Second Heaven is where the government under the Highest Heaven operates spiritually in the atmosphere where thrones, dominion, principalities, mountains and spiritual wickedness exist. The First Heaven is the physical sky and atmosphere along with the stars, moon, and sun. If these three realms of heaven are not aligned, then the fullness of the KINGDOM of God does not invade The Earth which is the physical realm that has its own government and mountains of influence.

The Sea (Marine Water KINGDOM) and the Realm of Hell (Fire) are other territories that must be battlegrounds where war must occur for the sake of the KINGDOM of God. Genesis 1 lets us know man was created to have dominion in the water. If the Marine KINGDOM is neglected or thought to be a fairy tale, destruction can occur in your life. Also, on another level, scripture let us know that the gates of hell will not prevail against the KINGDOM of God. So the fight at times is at the gates of hell where if we want to regain what the enemy has stolen from us in his trophy room, we must battle and fight. There are different territories we must think about when it comes to the KINGDOM of God. The war is a long term war that we must have a short term glance at by winning the battle for territories to become overcomers that inherit the KINGDOM of God down the road.

Dynamics of War

Some of us go about life just seeing ourselves as humans living our life day to day. We have families that live in communities where we read about current events. We live our lives where we might go to work or run a company. We might be part of a church where we go weekend by weekend to a place to hear a message to inspire us or grow in God. These things are part of regular life in the world but we have to understand that some of the things we are seeing in the world and living through is the effect of the war between the KINGDOM of God and the KINGDOM in darkness. Some of the bad we see in the world has us wondering to God why is it this bad? Part of the answer in part is because God has delegated authority and gifted us with the KINGDOM but we are not doing our part. The body of Christ has to see themselves as part of a KINGDOM and that they are in a war rather they realize or not.

This section is to look at certain dynamics so you can view and look at things from a lens of spiritual warfare. These dynamics of war are not just for the side of the KINGDOM of God but since these are rules and engagement of war that function from any angle, the enemy are utilizing these same dynamics.

Strategy & Planning

There is no way to win a war without strategy. This goes along with my KINGDOM buzz word "intention". When invoking strategy for the sake of the KINGDOM, we have to be intentional. Our Father has been very strategic in everything he does. He has a timing. He has a process. He is patient in the execution of his plan. There is a certain order that must be followed when it comes to which territories to go after first and subsequently. There is an understanding that there are some areas which are strongholds or strong fronts that must be taken first to secure other territories. Every territory is not the same so different tactics, weapons, and warfare must be invoked depending on the territory at hand. Strategy is key and pivotal in securing success in the war for the KINGDOM.

Where there is strategy, there is a plan. The plan is the what and the where. The strategy is the how and the when. If the vision and the plan is not in place then strategy has no place to sit. This puts me in mind of the game of chess which is known as the game of strategy. I am no way saying I am a master of chess but I realized from playing a number of times that when you start you need to have a goal and strategy in mind. You need to be some steps ahead of your opponent and account for the possible moves of your opponent. It is also good to have some contingency moves in hand as well.

Some of us are playing checkers when we should be playing chess. When this occurs we find ourselves on the defense the whole time. To some, this might sound complicated. But the good news is when you are on the side of the KINGDOM of God, Christ is the Commander in Chief already has a plan and strategy and we just have to align to it.

I also want to speak about war rooms that are needed to facilitate planning, strategy and counter measures during war. You better believe the enemy is being strategic in his quest to kill , steal, and destroy. The KINGDOM in darkness is organized and has strategic meetings on how the agenda of satan can be advanced. But know that our Father in heaven is the master strategist. I remember one time in prayer I had an encounter with an angel and I was taken to a place in heaven that the best way I can describe it was a strategic place for the KINGDOM of God. It was like something you would see in a Star Wars movie where it was this big structure where angels were coming in and out of, either to receive or execute orders. There were places inside of surveillance screens and like radar devices. There were councils where plans and strategy were being discussed. This encounter gave me great confidence in the KINGDOM and army of God.

Each side has scouts and watchmen. There are covert operations where intelligence is being gathered. Messengers are being sent to convey warning or next step instructions, Spiritual radar and sonar is utilized to gain intel. On God's side, you have men and women of God who are prophets and intercessors being aided and backed by the angels of God and strengthened by the Holy Spirit. But on the enemy's side, there are witches, warlocks, psychics, and sorcerers using different methods to communicate with satan and demons to execute his plan on the earth. The battle of strategies from both sides is in play. But the enemy is waging a war he has already lost. The

KINGDOM of God is very strategic and we have to change our perspective to be the same way as we maneuver in this life.

Occupy & Conquer

Another dynamic of war is the goal of each side to occupy what they already possess and also to gain more through every conquest. In war, things are not cordial but come with a mentality of me against them. In a sense, all games are disguised aspects of war. At the end of a game, just as war, there must be a victor or winner. So we can look at games and see aspects of war. Games have rules and protocols. Games come with ways to score or gain points. Also, offense and defense are important facets in games as well as war.

Offense from a game perspective is about scoring points and expanding the spread of the points you have over the points your opponents have. Defense is more about holding down the front and maintaining what you have while not letting the opponent take your territory or score points on you. A good defense is about having the right protection to stop the opponent whereas a good offense is having the right strategy and execution to be able to score in the opponent's territory. If it is football, basketball, baseball, soccer, boxing, fencing and the list can go on, it is simply war where offense and defense is at play.

The war in the KINGDOM of God is the same way. At a higher level, there are strategic things happening in the spiritual realm. In the earth realm, you as a believer have to know how to play a good offense and a good defense. Defense is to occupy that which is yours and offense is to conquer so you can add to what is yours. When we as believers change our perspective, we realize we can not just be still and do nothing because our current territory is at jeopardy and the expansion of our territory can be nullified. A citizen of the KINGDOM of God and as part of the royal bloodline you have to know how to occupy and conquer.

The Military

A component of the KINGDOM of God aligns with war is its military. So we can't talk about dynamics of war especially from a KINGDOM perspective without mentioning the military and weapons. The purpose of the military is to secure and defend the KINGDOM's or government's interests and also to deter war and fight in wars when needed. Without a military to support a KINGDOM, it will fall very quickly. Any effective KINGDOM must have a military.

We as believers like to say we are a part of the "army of the Lord" but in reality, the army is just one aspect of the military. There are many branches of the military and each KINGDOM or country needs all these branches because they have different duties and territories in which they operate. The military must be versatile and multi-faceted to cover all the intended territories. From a KINGDOM scope, we see that the KINGDOM has territories in the air (heaven), earth (land), and the water. Isn't it interesting that most countries or KINGDOMS have counterparts of their military for each of those same areas. They usually have an army, the marines, a navy, and an air force. I love to see movies from other cultures and I see the same pattern. If it is Nigeria, Britain, South Korea, Japan, China, India, or any other country, they will have these military branches.

The army's purpose is to defend and fight in the land spectrum when it comes to long term conflicts. Even if they are deployed to war on foreign land and the war is over, they are the branch who hangs around after for a while to make sure things stay in place. The marines' realm of protection is a mixture of the sea and sometimes land. Even though at times, they operate in the area of land, they are more for short term and crisis management when compared to the army. Because of this specialty their techniques are more geared for moving faster than the army to address more urgent needs. The navy's realm of influence is in the seas and oceans (water) where of course the air force handles the airways. Also, what I see in the U.S. is that there is emphasis on the borders with homeland security where you have the National Guard handling the borders on land and the Coast Guards handling the borders in the water. A good military must have strategic fronts in every territory of interest.

The KINGDOM of God and the KINGDOM in darkness has military entities on all territories when it comes to earth, the heavenlies, and the water. The military is very organized on both sides when it comes to hierarchy and rank. On one side you have angels and KINGDOM believers where on the other side you have fallen angels, demons, and human agents (witches, warlocks, etc.) These operatives are stationed in the aforementioned territories. You have those who are unaware of the war who are civilians. Military networks are also in place along with enemies and allies.

I have mentioned that there is a hierarchy based on rank. The higher ranks are more involved in the strategy where the lower ranks are more so those who take and follow the orders. Another caveat is that there are different skill levels and also groups known as special forces. Each branch of the military has its own area of special forces. The Navy has Navy Seals. The Army has the Rangers, Night Stalkers, and Green Berets. The Air Force has pararescue specialists, combat controllers and weather forecasters. And the marines have Raiders and RECON units. In every military branch these special operation forces had to undergo major and intense training to be the best of the best to be assigned special places and endure conditions that the majority can't handle. I likened these in the KINGDOM of God to KINGDOM apostles, prophets, intercessors, spiritual warriors and watchmen. Some understand how to combat witchcraft (earth and air) while some specialty is to oppose the marine KINGDOM. On the enemy side, these are witch doctors, high priest/priestess of the occult, sorcerers, wizards, and high degreed masonic individuals.

Intelligence

The KINGDOM of God is a spiritual KINGDOM and the war is fought from a spiritual perspective. Some of you all's spiritual eyes might have not ever been opened and you might doubt the existence of things like demons, angels, dragons and things like that. But they do exist just like the existence of the Father, Christ, heaven, and hell.

I have been at times blessed to have my spiritual eyes opened and I have observed a number of angels. They differ in size, appearance, glory, and power. Some angels have wings and some don't. Some have brighter light than others. Some have a masculine appearance and some a female appearance. Some might carry swords while others handle a shofar, scroll, and books. My point for bringing this up is that not all those involved in the war do the same thing, have the same rank, or even the same operations. Some angels are warrior angels. Others are messenger angels. Some gather intel and record things in a book for a witness and testimony. They are not at all fighting with swords. Do you remember the story in the book of Daniel where Daniel was seeking the Lord for 21 days? In this story, Gabriel the messenger angel came and he let Daniel know he had to wait on Michael, a warring angel to help clear the way. There are different duties but intelligence is needed.

There are some aspects of intelligence gathering that we have to consider. In the U.S., there is a network of intelligence agencies that work with the other branches at times. You have the Central Intelligence Agency (CIA) and the Federal Bureau of Investigation (FBI). The CIA focuses on gathering intel and eliminating threats from a foreign perspective and the FBI gathers intel and does investigation for items within the country. Also, there is the Secret service who are doing the same for the protection of the President, Cabinet and other high ranking officials and their families. Besides having a plan, strategy, and armed agents for war, intelligence and a network to communicate that intel is a very needed dynamic of war. In the KINGDOM of God, I see the ability of KINGDOM believers to be led by the Holy Spirit key to receiving intelligence to have an edge over the enemy. Also,

KINGDOM prophets that have the ability of sight and revelation helps in this area as well.

Weapons of War

> *4 (**For the weapons of our warfare are not carnal**, but **mighty through God to the pulling down of strong holds;**) 5 Casting down imaginations, and every high thing that exalteth itself against the knowledge of God, and bringing into captivity every thought to the obedience of Christ; (2 Corinthians 10:4-5)*

Another dynamic of war I wanted to cover is weapons. The aforementioned scriptures clearly show that for strongholds to be pulled down, high things to be brought down low and to bring other territories into captivity, weapons of war must be employed. The weapons that bring victory in this spiritual war can't be of this world. They can't be carnal. This is a spiritual war and they must be spiritual weapons. We can't use weapons of our own power and strength or of the flesh but we have to use the ones issued by our King , the Commander in Chief. The enemy is using weapons of the past, accusations, lies, hate, fear and lust. But our weapons that are mighty as believers are the Word of God, faith, truth, prayer, love, fasting, and the blood of the Lamb.

There are many different weapons in nature. There are guns, knives, swords, grenades, bows with arrows, bombs, and even chemical weapons to name a few. And with each weapon there is a strategy and a specific place where and when to use it. Some weapons require ammunition and have to be reloaded and restocked. Like each military branch has a different territory they are protecting and assigned to, they also have their different types of weapons and vehicles they use to be effective in their specified arenas. We as believers must first be skilled and trained with our weapons. Then we need to understand where the King has us posted and understand the assignment. We need to know when to use which weapons and when not to. Then there is a part of discipline and assessment of inventory that has to be employed to make sure that weapons are clean or sharp and that we have all the bullets, clips, or other ammunition needed on the battlefield. KINGDOM believers must be skilled and wise when it comes to weaponry to help the King of Kings advance his KINGDOM.

The KINGDOM Intention in War

> Then **cometh the end**, when he shall have delivered up the KINGDOM to God, even the Father; when he shall have put down all rule and all authority and power. For he must reign, till he hath put all enemies under his feet. The last enemy that shall be destroyed is death. For he hath put all things under his feet. But when he saith all things are put under him, it is manifest that he is excepted, which did put all things under him. And when all things shall be subdued unto him, then shall the Son also himself be subject unto him that put all things under him, that **God may be all in all**. (I Corinthians 15:24-28)

The purpose and intention of this KINGDOM war from the perspective of the Father is not just to war and battle for the fun of it. The Father's whole objective is to be all in all. When it comes to the endgame of the KINGDOM of God, the Father's desire is to expand the KINGDOM in every area of demonic rule and darkness and fill it all with him, his rule and light. He wants a KINGDOM domain, world, and age without end. The KINGDOM of God will continue to be at war and be violent against darkness, emptiness, disobedience, and non-compliance. This is a KINGDOM , not a democracy or anarchy.

In Genesis, we see an earth empty and without void. I believe this was due to an already rebellion by the enemy and so the Father decides to rebuild the earth with man made in his image to replenish the earth. He does not tell Adam and Eve just to be fruitful and multiply but to replenish which means to bring back to its former glory. But then Adam falls and the second Adam, the ram in the bush, Christ our Messiah came to redeem the world so the KINGDOM will not be lost. God's creation is vast and the whole of creation, bigger than just earth, is groaning the manifestations of the Sons of God. As we mature into the KINGDOM of Sons that the Father is looking for , then the KINGDOM will continue to expand to earth, other planets, galaxies and dimensions throughout eternity. (I know that might be a lot to take in and I might have wrecked some of you all theologies.)

When Adam sinned and ate of that forbidden tree, the authority and power laid upon Adam as a KINGDOM Son was then delivered to satan since he was the one who tricked him out of his birthright. This is the same principle when Jacob "the supplanter" tricked Esau out of his birthright and then afterward possessed the position. In this, satan could call himself the god of this world and therefore blinded the world with a lie. satan even offered Christ the KINGDOMS of the world because he said they were delivered unto him. Who gave him these KINGDOMS? Adam did. But Christ took the keys of the KINGDOM and gave it to his body. The enemy does not want to relinquish his position and that is why the war is occurring. Now it is our duty to the King to war, overcome the enemy in every way, and expand the KINGDOM of God. This is his intention as we war to inherit the KINGDOM and all its territories.

Chapter 5 : It's All About The KINGDOM

In previous chapters, it was highlighted that the Most High's intention was the KINGDOM from the beginning. The purpose of this chapter is to illustrate that not only was it his agenda from the beginning but also that this message was intertwined in the law, the prophets and all throughout the New Testament part of the bible. Hopefully, after this chapter you will be able to see that the thread of the fabric of the whole bible is the KINGDOM of God. We see in Christendom today, a lot of focus on hyper grace, programs to draw the masses, and various other topics. But the message that is dear to the heart of the Father that he wants to hear echoed all over the world for all generations is the message and good news of the KINGDOM. In his eyes, it is all about the KINGDOM. So let's take a journey from Genesis to Revelation and see if there are any hints or implications about the KINGDOM of God throughout the whole of the bible.

Adam & Eve (Genesis)

And God said, Let us make man in our image, after our likeness: and
let them have dominion *over the fish of the sea, and over the fowl of*
the air, and over the cattle, and over all the earth, and over every
creeping thing that creepeth upon the earth. (Genesis 1:26)

The Father's reason for making mankind was to have an offspring in his image who lived on the earth and had dominion (kingship) over every realm. This speaks to the KINGDOM mindset of the Father. He wanted an offspring that had his image and likeness who could be like him. We know that the Father and Christ have thrones which are in line with the concept of Kings and their KINGDOM. Christ is the King of kings. The intention was for Christ to be the highest ranking "king" over the "kings" that he is calling us to be. The whole dream of the Father was to have a royal family who ruled and reigned in harmony together over the heavens, the air, the sea, and the earth. A huge KINGDOM of kings was the beautiful picture in the mind of the Father.

Adam and Eve was supposed to be the start and catalyst of this super KINGDOM but through disobedience they lost the image and nature to rule and reign this KINGDOM and the enemy was able to take the reins and do his bidding till man was renewed to overcome him. The Great Father of Heaven in his foreknowledge and wisdom proclaimed something powerful in Genesis 3 which I see as a proclamation of the good news of a coming KINGDOM.

*And I will put enmity between thee and the woman, and between **thy***
seed** and **her seed**; it shall **bruise thy head**, and thou shalt **bruise his
***heel**. (Genesis 2:15)*

These were words given by the Father about the serpent and the woman. It was about two bloodlines (seed); one that was of the enemy and flesh and one that was of the Spirit through the womb of a woman. One seed would crush and defeat the other seed. The term "head" speaks to kingship so after the fall of Adam and Eve, the enemy held a seat of "head" in this physical world. But the good news and the gospel is that one day through the bloodline of mankind would come a seed that will crush the KINGDOM in darkness and that KINGDOM in darkness would be the footstool of the KINGDOM of Christ. Christ will strike a blow to the head of the enemy and the enemy will just bruise the heel of the Christ (the cross). This KINGDOM prophecy was released in the earth waiting for its fulfillment. It's all about the KINGDOM.

Enoch & Noah

> *These are the generations of Noah: Noah was **a just man and perfect in his generations**, and Noah walked with God.(Genesis 6:9)*

I know some stray away from the topic of Enoch and especially the book of Enoch. But the canon of the bible we know in these modern times refers to the book of Enoch many times. It also speaks to the character of Enoch so much that his testimony with God was that he pleased him. The Father was so pleased that God translated him and brought him in the spiritual realm away from the earth. The reason for the mention of Enoch was that during his time there were some Watchers (angels) who left their first estate to defile women and birthed from these women were giants also known as the Nephilim. I believe that the intention of the fallen Watchers was to muddy the bloodlines so that the King and Savior could not come forth per the KINGDOM proclamation that was released in Genesis 3.

Per the book of Enoch and other parts of Genesis, Enoch was chosen to release words of judgment to the fallen Watchers. Enoch was also shown that through the violence in the earth and corruption of the bloodline of mankind that the Most High will send a deluge (flood) to the earth. But the Father, always having a ram in the bush, selected Noah, a descendant of Enoch, who was perfect in his genealogy and whose bloodline was pure to survive the flood and keep the bloodline going. There needed to be two factors for the purpose of who would go in the ark. They had to be just and they had to be perfect in their generations (bloodline). The flood and the ark was all set in motion for the sake of the KINGDOM of the Most High. It's all about the KINGDOM.

Abraham, Isaac, and Jacob

> 5 *Neither shall thy name any more be called Abram, but thy name shall be Abraham; for a father of many nations have I made thee.* 6 *And I will make thee exceeding fruitful, and I will make nations of thee, and* **kings shall come out of thee**. 7 *And I will establish my covenant between me and thee and* **thy seed** *after thee in their generations for an* **everlasting covenant**, *to be a God unto thee, and to thy seed after thee.*
> (Genesis 17:5-7)

The continuance of the KINGDOM bloodline did not stop with Noah. It continued until the Most High made a covenant with Abram in Genesis 17. He changed his name to Abraham which means "a father of many nations". Isn't a father (bloodline) of many nations for many generations definitely an indicator that points to a KINGDOM or dynasty? In verse 6 of that chapter Abraham is told that "kings" will come out of him. This definitely was an everlasting KINGDOM covenant that the Most High made with Abraham. "KINGDOM" was God's intention as even with Isaac and Jacob, he re-established that covenant with these two with a KINGDOM perspective.

It's all about the KINGDOM.

Moses, Israel and the Feasts of the Most High

*5 Now therefore, if ye will obey my voice indeed, and keep my covenant, then ye shall be a peculiar treasure unto me above all people: for all the earth is mine: 6 And **ye shall be unto me a KINGDOM of priests**, and an holy nation. These are the words which thou shalt speak unto the children of Israel. (Exodus 19:5-6)*

In Exodus 19, the KINGDOM motif continues when the Most High begin to re-establish a covenant with the children of Israel through Moses. In verse 6, he lets Moses know that his intention is for Israel to be a KINGDOM of priests that would be peculiar and set apart for him. The law given to Moses (the first five books) all pointed to Christ and his KINGDOM. This was the goal and endgame of the Most High for Israel to be a physical picture in the world of a KINGDOM of God until the fullness of Christ came to usher in the new covenant and everlasting KINGDOM.

Even the feasts and the Levitical priesthood pointed to KINGDOM things. In the Holy of Holies, you have the mercy seat which is the throne of God (KINGDOM). And with the feasts of the LORD, you have seven feasts that outline the journey of God with man so God can establish his bloodline and KINGDOM in the earth. You have Passover which symbolizes Christ as the Passover lamb to be a sin offering to blot out our sins to gain access to the KINGDOM. Then the feast of Unleavened Bread that points to the leaven of the enemy being taken away from us so we can eat the living bread of our King. Then next you the feast of Sheaf of Firstfruits that signifies the resurrection of the Messiah and him being the first fruit of the KINGDOM of God that will continue to grow in harvest. This leads us to the feast of

Pentecost which means 50 days after Passover to signify that after a time of the cross, will come a time where the believers in Christ will be empowered with power from on high to be witnesses of Christ and his KINGDOM.

Then you have the three fall feasts starting with the feast of Trumpets that signifies the next coming of the Lord in the clouds with a sound of a trumpet to further establish his KINGDOM. After this coming, the judgment is set which is what Atonement is about where the blood of Christ has reconciled us and brought us back to oneness with the Father. Atonement means at - one - ment, the act of making one and bringing them together. And here the judgment will be who will be allowed further into the KINGDOM of God. And the final feast is Tabernacles, is the consummation of the KINGDOM where the theme is oneness, and rest and where God will be our King and we will be his people and there will be no end to this KINGDOM. We will dwell under the tents and tabernacles with the Father and Christ because they will be our light and temple. The final feast shows a picture of kings and priests (tabernacles) under the highest Kings , the Father and his Son. It's all about the KINGDOM.

Major and Minor Prophets

From Moses and the law part of the bible to the Major and Minor prophets, the books in between were about the KINGDOM. It might not seem like it outright even though two of those books are First and Second Kings. And another two books, First and Second Chronicles, paralleled the books of Kings as it chronicled the genealogy of the kings of Israel. But these books were tracking the royal kingship bloodline of Christ. Did you realize that Ruth was the ancestor of King David and Christ? These are not just books of the bible telling cute little stories. They are strategically placed there. These are books that are tracking a bloodline and declaring a KINGDOM. So in this section we will look at the prophets and some examples where they were prophesying about an everlasting KINGDOM that would come to the earth.

King David

I know what some are thinking. Why are we talking about King David in the part about prophets? The reason is because King David was a prophet. He was a forerunner and saw many things concerning Christ and the KINGDOM. Here are a few references from the book of Psalms in which King David authored:

> *Thy throne, O God, is for ever and ever: the sceptre of **thy KINGDOM** is a right sceptre. (Psalms 45.6)*

> *The Lord hath prepared his throne in the heavens; and **his KINGDOM** ruleth over all. (Psalms 103:19)*

> ***Thy KINGDOM is an everlasting KINGDOM**, and **thy dominion** endureth throughout all generations. (Psalms 145:13)*

> ***8** Who is this **King of glory**? The Lord strong and mighty, the Lord mighty in battle. **9** Lift up your heads, O ye gates; even lift them up, ye everlasting doors; and **the King of glory** shall come in. **10** Who is this **King of glory**? The Lord of hosts, he is **the King of glory**. Selah.(Psalms 24:8-10)*

The previous scriptures are just a few that are outlined in the Psalms where King David highlights the greatness of the Most High's KINGDOM and how is a mighty King. He points out that this KINGDOM is one of righteousness and that the throne of God is in the heavens and rules over all. This KINGDOM is one of dominion that is everlasting to endure through all generations. Not only this, but the KINGDOM of the Most High is one of glory where the King of glory will come in and be strong and mighty in battle (war). King David definitely had the KINGDOM of God in mind when he declared these things in the book of Psalms. It's all about the KINGDOM.

Daniel

> And **the KINGDOM** and dominion, and the greatness of **the KINGDOM** under the whole heaven, shall be given to the people of the saints of the most High, **whose KINGDOM** is an **everlasting KINGDOM**, and **all dominions** shall serve and obey him. (Daniel 7:27)

Another prophet, Daniel, in the seventh chapter of the book of Daniel, had dreams and night visions that showed that four earthly KINGDOMS would rise but the Ancient of Days will eventually give power to the Son of Man to destroy these KINGDOMS and from there the saints of the Most High will be able to possess the KINGDOM of God. This is one of my favorite KINGDOM chapters in the whole of the bible. Daniel the prophet is prophesying about the KINGDOM of Christ and its expansion in the future. It's all about the KINGDOM.

Isaiah

> 6 For unto us a child is born, unto us a son is given: and **the government** shall be upon his shoulder: and his name shall be called Wonderful, Counsellor, The mighty God, The everlasting Father, The Prince of Peace. 7 Of the **increase of his government** and peace there shall be no end, upon the throne of David, and upon **his KINGDOM**, to order it, and to establish it with judgment and with justice from henceforth even for ever. The zeal of the Lord of hosts will perform this. (Isaiah 9:6-7)

Isaiah the prophet continues in the tune that declares the arrival of Christ the King whose KINGDOM will have no end. In one of the chapters of this great book known as the book of Isaiah, he declares a natural child would be born of a woman on the earth but in reality a Son from above would be given to us. The verse goes on to proclaim that the government (the KINGDOM) will be upon the shoulders of this child and he will go by the names of Wonderful, Counsellor, The Mighty God, and Everlasting Father. And the increase of the KINGDOM will no know no end and it will be established with judgment and justice hence the name "Counsellor" which is a legal term for judge or lawyer. And then it seals it with the statement that the zeal and intention of the Most High will definitely perform this. In other words, there is no stopping this thing called the KINGDOM. This is just one set of scriptures that relate to the message of the KINGDOM by Isaiah. But Isaiah knew that it was and is all about the KINGDOM.

John the Baptist

> *1 In those days came **John the Baptist**, preaching in the wilderness of Judaea, 2 And saying, **Repent ye: for the KINGDOM of heaven is at hand**. 3 For this is he that was spoken of by the prophet Esaias (Isaiah), saying, The voice of one crying in the wilderness, Prepare ye the way of the Lord, make his paths straight.(Matthew 3:1-3)*

John the Baptist, another prophet, comes on the scene and what does he do after years of people talking about and wondering about the KINGDOM of God? He proclaims that the KINGDOM of Heaven (God) is at hand. He proclaimed and preached that the KINGDOM was coming on the scene. I did not put John the Baptist in the previous section of Major and Minor Prophets because he was the bridge of the old into the new. Christ said he was the greatest prophet until that time. Why? He did not do any miracles but what he did is that he sounded the alarm and declared the KINGDOM of God. His message and prophecy was simple. It was about the KINGDOM of God.

For continuity's sake, the previously discussed prophet Isaiah actually prophesied about John the Baptist and says that he will be the voice of one crying in the wilderness and that he would prepare the way for the living Christ. John the Baptist, the one who people thought was strange out in the wilderness and who was filled with the Holy Spirit in his mother's womb had a very important mandate. This mandate was to be a witness and forerunner of the KINGDOM's message that eventually Christ will take over and proclaim for he was the fulfillment of that message. It's all about the KINGDOM.

Christ the King

He must increase, but I must decrease. (John 3:30)

So John the Baptist, the cousin of Christ, comes on the scene with an emphatic KINGDOM message to prepare the way for Christ. John the Baptist was the appetizer but Christ was the main course so much so that John the Baptist knew that his purpose was fulfilled and he had to diminish so the increase of Christ and his KINGDOM could come forth just like Isaiah said in Isaiah chapter 9. He baptized Christ and Christ went to the wilderness to be tempted by the enemy and returned in power to proclaim the message of the KINGDOM. John the Baptist had a wilderness ministry but Christ overcame the enemy in the wilderness and was released from the wilderness in power to release and expand the KINGDOM's message to the world.

*From that time **Jesus began to preach**, and to say, **Repent: for the KINGDOM of heaven is at hand**. (Matthew 4:17)*

And from the time Christ came from the wilderness, he began to echo and proclaim the same thing word for word what John the Baptist proclaimed, "Repent, for the KINGDOM of heaven is at hand". And if you follow the scripture in the Gospels, you will see everywhere he went he preached and taught about the KINGDOM of God. It was the main topic of everything he talked about. The Beatitudes were about the KINGDOM of God. Blessed is the meek for theirs is the KINGDOM of God. And then all of his parables were about the KINGDOM of God. Even when he gave an example of how we should pray, it demonstrated that we should pray and command for the KINGDOM of God to come. In chapters five through seven in Matthew, also known as the Sermon on the Mount, this was like a manifesto or constitution of the KINGDOM of God being taught to the masses. In the same sermon, he in Matthew 6 said that the first thing to seek above anything else is the KINGDOM of God. Why? Because it's all about the KINGDOM of God.

*5 These **twelve Jesus sent forth**, and commanded them, saying, Go not into the way of the Gentiles, and into any city of the Samaritans enter ye not: 6 But go rather to the lost sheep of the house of Israel. 7 And as ye **go, preach, saying, The KINGDOM of heaven is at hand.** (Matthew 10:5-7)*

Not only did John the Baptist preach the KINGDOM of God, but then Christ Jesus came and did the same. But it did not stop there. Christ then anoints and tells the twelve apostles to do it and then later he sends seventy other disciples to proclaim the same thing, "The KINGDOM of heaven is at hand." See all those before John the Baptist only prophesied that the KINGDOM was coming but from John the Baptist on, the scripture lets us know that mankind then began to press into the KINGDOM of God. And they began to press into the KINGDOM because the message went from being prophesied to being proclaimed. The KINGDOM message had to continue.

*To whom also he (Christ) shewed himself alive after his passion by many infallible proofs, being seen of them forty days, and **speaking of the things pertaining to the KINGDOM of God**: (Acts 1:3)*

Even after the death and the resurrection of Christ, leading up to his ascension to the Father, Christ spent forty days with the disciples. This was not to have a good time of fellowship. This was not them just sitting around having random conversation. No, this was intentional teaching pertaining to the KINGDOM of God. And for something to be discussed for three and a half years to his disciples and then for forty more days before his ascension to me is very telling of the importance of the message of the KINGDOM. Christ since he first came on the scene was about one thing, the message and the gospel of the KINGDOM of God. It's all about the KINGDOM.

Apostle James

*Hearken, my beloved brethren, Hath not God chosen the poor of this world rich in faith, and **heirs of the KINGDOM** which he hath promised to them that love him? (James 2:5)*

The twelve apostles were commissioned and sent to proclaim (preach) the gospel of the KINGDOM. We see this from the previous scripture that Apostle James declared the KINGDOM of God and his teaching was from that KINGDOM perspective. I want to take a moment to say that in our times, there are many who proclaim that they are apostles but I want to add if they are not talking or declaring the KINGDOM of God, then they are false. One of the main purposes of the apostle in the church of Christ is to go to regions and territories and proclaim the KINGDOM of God. Remember, it's all about the KINGDOM of God.

Apostle Peter

> *For so an entrance shall be ministered unto you abundantly **into the everlasting KINGDOM of our Lord and Saviour Jesus Christ**. (2 Peter 1:11)*

In the aforementioned verse, we see Apostle Peter ministering to the readers of his Second Epistle about the KINGDOM of God. He in this scripture is actually declaring that the proclamation of the good news of the KINGDOM actually creates an opening or entrance so we can walk in the abundance of the everlasting KINGDOM of our Lord and Savior Jesus Christ. It's all about the KINGDOM of God.

Apostle Paul

Paul in the Book of Acts

> *20 Howbeit, as the disciples stood round about him, he rose up, and came into the city: and the next day he departed with Barnabas to Derbe. 21 And when they had preached the gospel to that city, and had taught many, they returned again to Lystra, and to Iconium, and Antioch, 22 Confirming the souls of the disciples, and exhorting them to continue in the faith, and that we must through much tribulation **enter into the KINGDOM of God**. (Acts 14:20-22)*

> *And he went into the synagogue, and spake boldly for the space of three*

*months, disputing and persuading the things **concerning the KINGDOM of God**. (Acts 19:8)*

*And now, behold, I know that ye all, among whom I have gone **preaching the KINGDOM of God**, shall see my face no more. (Acts 20:25)*

__30__ And Paul dwelt two whole years in his own hired house, and received all that came in unto him, __31 Preaching the KINGDOM of God,__ and teaching those things which concern the Lord Jesus Christ, with all confidence, no man forbidding him. (Acts 28:30-31)

The Book of Acts highlights many wonderful aspects of how Christ and the apostles did many mighty things. But what it also reveals was what the emphasis of Paul's teaching and preaching was. In the previously mentioned scriptures we see that Apostle Paul made disciples who he encouraged to continue in the faith through tribulation to enter the KINGDOM of God. In Acts 19:8, Apostle Paul taught in the synagogue for a space of three months where the teaching and disputings were about the one and only KINGDOM of God. Then in the end of the book of Acts we see that Paul lived in a particular house for two years where his first priority was preaching the KINGDOM of God with all confidence. Paul, like the others, valued the gospel of the KINGDOM. It's all about the KINGDOM of God!!!

Paul in His Epistles

*__9__ Know ye not that the unrighteous shall not **inherit the KINGDOM of God**? Be not deceived: neither fornicators, nor idolaters, nor adulterers, nor effeminate, nor abusers of themselves with mankind, __10__ Nor thieves, nor covetous, nor drunkards, nor revilers, nor extortioners, shall i**nherit the KINGDOM of God**. (1 Corinthians 6:9-10)*

*Now this I say, brethren, that flesh and blood cannot **inherit the KINGDOM of God**; neither doth corruption inherit incorruption. (1 Corinthians 15:50)*

*Who hath delivered us from the power of darkness, and hath translated us into the **KINGDOM of his dear Son**: (Colossians 1:13)*

Apostle Paul, outside of what we read concerning him, in the book of Acts, we were also blessed with his epistles (letters) that he wrote. In his epistles he always made mention of the KINGDOM of God and how the main goal was to "inherit" the KINGDOM of God. He also declared that the unrighteous would not inherit the KINGDOM of God and those who do certain things which he listed would not qualify. There is a difference in believing in the sacrifice of Christ so you can go to heaven when you die and striving for maturity and righteousness for the purpose to inherit the KINGDOM of God. Also, in 1 Corinthians 15, we know that flesh and blood can't inherit the KINGDOM while in the first chapter of Colossians, Paul encourages his readers that we have been delivered out of darkness and transferred to the KINGDOM of Christ. These tones of KINGDOM verbiage are throughout the epistles of Apostle Paul. It's all about the KINGDOM of God.

Apostle Philip

*But when they believed **Philip preaching the things concerning the KINGDOM of God**, and the name of Jesus Christ, they were baptized, both men and women. (Acts 8:12)*

Apostle Philip, who I believe is forgotten sometimes in the scriptures compared to some other apostles, also believed in the preaching of the gospel of the KINGDOM of God. It was many men and women who came into relationship with Christ by Philip preaching things specifically concerning the KINGDOM. This is the same apostle who also in the book of Acts preached to the eunuch and after he baptized him was translated to another part of the world supernaturally. I believe it is safe to assume that Philip preached Christ and his KINGDOM to the eunuch as he was taught earlier by Christ's example and discipling. Why? Because it is all about the KINGDOM.

The Book of Hebrews

*But unto the Son he saith, Thy throne, O God, is for ever and ever: a sceptre of righteousness is **the sceptre of thy KINGDOM**. (Hebrews 1:8)*

*Wherefore we **receiving a KINGDOM** which cannot be moved, let us have grace, whereby we may serve God acceptably with reverence and godly fear: (Hebrews 12:28)*

The Book of Hebrews which some debate the authorship of this book also contains language concerning the KINGDOM of God. This great book which speaks to Hebrews about the symbolism of the Levitical priesthood and the things of the law of Moses. In the first chapter, the author of the book of Hebrews declares Christ as the Son of God who has a throne and holds a scepter of righteousness in his hand. This declaration confirms the prophetic declaration that King David in the Psalms made concerning our Christ and King. And also, in chapter 12, the author elaborates more that we have received a KINGDOM that cannot and ever be moved. He continues in connection with this KINGDOM for the readers to serve God with revenge and godly fear to be acceptable. Acceptable for what? You already know it is the KINGDOM. Here is another book of the bible that highlights the theme of the KINGDOM. It's all about the KINGDOM.

Apostle John and the Book of Revelation

*I John, who also am your brother, and companion in tribulation, and **in the KINGDOM and patience of Jesus Christ**, was in the isle that is called Patmos, for the word of God, and for the testimony of Jesus Christ. (Revelation 1:9)*

*And I heard a loud voice saying in heaven, Now is come salvation, and strength, **and the KINGDOM of our God,** and the power of his Christ: for the accuser of our brethren is cast down, which accused them before our God day and night. (Revelation 12:10)*

Christ is the beginning and the end. So just as Christ was in the beginning and the ending, his KINGDOM is mentioned on some level also in the first and last book of the canon of the bible. In Genesis, the hope and call of a KINGDOM is evident and in the book of Revelation written by Apostle John the Beloved, the topic is kicked off in the first chapter of this epistle to the seven churches. John introduces himself as a brother and companion in tribulation in the KINGDOM of Jesus Christ. Also in those chapters, he alludes to himself and the readers that Christ has made them kings and priests. And in chapter 12, which I believe is one of the climaxes of the book of Revelation, a loud voice is heard in heaven saying now salvation has come and also the KINGDOM of our God has defeated the devil and his false KINGDOM in darkness. We have heard people say, "In the end, we win". The book of Revelation ends with the KINGDOM of God being triumphant and the KINGDOMS of this world being defeated. From Genesis to Revelation, it's all about the KINGDOM.

KINGDOM Timeline

The bible followed the KINGDOM bloodline and the establishment of the KINGDOM.

- Adam was to rule and have dominion in every realm.
- Abraham was told kings will come out of him that will bless the earth (Gen. 17).
- Moses was told Israel was to be a KINGDOM of priests (Ex. 19).
- The Major and Minor prophets prophesied about the KINGDOM.
- David in Psalms (the King of Glory was declared and an everlasting KINGDOM)
- Daniel (Ch. 7) - the saints will possess the KINGDOM and it will have no end
- Isaiah (Ch. 9) - a Son would be given and the increase of his government (KINGDOM) would have no end.
- John the Baptist preached and proclaimed the KINGDOM.
- The Messiah preached and proclaimed the KINGDOM.
- The disciples (apostles) were told to preach and proclaim the KINGDOM. (Matthew 10:7)
- It is this message and good news or the gospel of the KINGDOM that signs and wonders manifested to confirm.
- The Messiah's parables were all about the KINGDOM.
- The parable of the sower about the "word of the KINGDOM".
- After Jesus resurrected, he spent 40 days with the disciples talking ONLY about the KINGDOM.
- Mathew 5-7 is the Constitution of the KINGDOM that house the commandments of Christ Jesus (Yeshua)
- Beatitudes are all about the KINGDOM of God. (Matt. 5)
- Whoever does "these" commandments will be great in the KINGDOM. (Matthew 5)

- Even the heartbeat of our prayers should be that his KINGDOM comes. (Matthew 6)
- Asking, seeking, and knocking is all about the KINGDOM.
- It is the KINGDOM and his righteousness that we should be seeking first before anything. (Matthew 6)
- Enter in at the strait and narrow gate that leads to life and his KINGDOM. (Matt. 7)
- Paul, James, Peter, John, Philip and others declared the KINGDOM of God.
- The book of Revelation is the revealing of Christ as a King and the declaration of the KINGDOM of God taking over the KINGDOMS of this world.
- Now we are in the KINGDOM Age.

The theme of the KINGDOM is the heartbeat of the bible.

Chapter 6 : The Gospel of the KINGDOM

*And **this gospel of the KINGDOM** shall be preached in all the world*
for a witness unto all nations (Matthew 24:14)

When it comes to the things pertaining to the Most High, it is indeed all about the KINGDOM of God. One thing that a great KINGDOM needs is a very functional network of communication. With any government there are new programs and laws being put in place and there has to be a way to get the awareness of these changes out to the public. When it comes to communication in the KINGDOM of God, you need a King, his proclamations, and KINGDOM ambassadors to spread the news of his proclamations and decrees. The KINGDOM believers are the ambassadors of the proclamation of the gospel of the KINGDOM of God. There is a message that is coming from the throne room of the Most High that he wants to invade every territory and every region. And that message is the announcement and demonstration of the KINGDOM of God.

Proclamations and announcements from a King is not something we should take lightly. I think of the times in scripture when the Most High does not want us to add or take away from his words. So when it comes to a decree or proclamation that has been signed, sealed, and ready to be delivered, whoever the messenger is should not be trying to reword it, add to it, or take away from it.

Have you ever been to an event and someone is being honored and there is a proclamation from the president, governor, or mayor? If you have, then you know this is not something to be taken lightly. The person announcing the proclamation does not skim over it. The person does not put it in their own words. The person does not decide not to read it at all or reveal it. But usually what should happen is that the ambassador there on behalf of the higher official should read the proclamation in its entirety with the exact wording that was released from the chief executive in that scenario which in our context is the King of Kings. Why? Because there is a particular language of the King and his KINGDOM.

The gospel of the KINGDOM of God is definitely such a proclamation where we should treat as the King desires in the official language of the KINGDOM. The gospel of the KINGDOM is something through the years that has been misunderstood, mishandled, communicated wrongly, or watered down. A lot of focus of what is called the "gospel" is centered about the death, burial, and resurrection with the reward of heaven and not around the covenant and promise of the KINGDOM. We need balance in this and have all of the parts of the gospel explained and proclaimed. The word "Gospel" means good news or glad tidings. And if we are using the phrase "gospel of the KINGDOM" then what we proclaimed should be in alignment to the good news or glad tidings of the KINGDOM. Which KINGDOM? The KINGDOM of GOD!!!!

Looking through the bible we see the gospel mentioned a number times in different contexts. In one place you see "the gospel of Jesus Christ" or maybe "gospel of his Son". This is not the gospel about Christ and the Son but the gospel which Christ and the Son preached. Another reference might use "the gospel of the grace of God" or "the gospel of peace". "Everlasting gospel" is mentioned in the scriptures in some places. And then lastly you have the term "gospel of the KINGDOM" featured in the book of Matthew and Mark in connection with Christ. I have heard some teach that there are different phases of the gospel. But I don't adhere to that because the intention of the Father has been the same since the beginning. He has declared the end from the beginning and these different terms are all the same thing just from different facets. The gospel of the KINGDOM is everlasting. It is one that brings grace and peace to the hearers. Also, the who and the main character of the gospel is Jesus Christ (Yeshua) the King. The good news that the Father wants out of the bag is for people to have awareness of his KINGDOM.

The True Meaning of Preaching

I come from a religious background where the term "preaching" insinuates a person who hoops, hollers, jumps up and down, and who electrifies the crowd with their theatrics and skills of presentation. And after that, the crowds walk out from the service saying to one another, "He sure did preach.". They walked out excited but spiritually empty and unchanged. Preaching in these modern times, has the connotation of someone riled up with fiery energy and passion. But let's look at the Greek meaning of the word "preach" in the context of the scriptures.

The Greek word for "preach" is the word "kerysso" and it means to be a herald, to preach, proclaim or publish. When I think of the word "herald", I think of the Christmas song, "Hark, the Herald Angel Sing". In this song, the lyrics starts off with, "Hark, the Herald Angel Sing, "Glory to the new born King, peace on earth...." So in the context of this song we see that the angel who is acting as a herald is declaring and proclaiming something. A preacher should be a person who is proclaiming something. They should be making an announcement. They should be pointing to an already packaged message from the King.

The gospel of the KINGDOM is not to be taught but it to be preached and proclaimed and published. Yes, there might be teaching to bring more understanding of what the KINGDOM of God is BUT the gospel should declare a who, what, when, where, and how. It should be declaring that the KINGDOM of the Most High is on the scene and bring with it good news. There is a lot happening in the name of "preaching" but at times nothing is being proclaimed. I am here to tell you as you read this that the gospel, good news, and glad tidings of the KINGDOM must be preached and proclaimed.

Sent and Heard

*13 For whosoever shall call upon the name of the Lord shall be saved. 14 How then shall they call on him in whom they have not believed? and how shall they believe in him of **whom they have not heard**? and how shall they hear **without a preacher**? 15 And how shall they preach, **except they be sent**? as it is written, How beautiful are the feet of them that **preach the gospel of peace**, and bring glad tidings of good things! (Romans 10:13-15)*

The gospel of the KINGDOM should not only be preached but it must be preached by someone who has specifically been tasked to proclaim the KINGDOM. If they are not sent, how can they preach and be effective so people can truly hear from the ears of their heart. According to Romans 10, the progression is that someone is sent. Then the sent someone preaches the gospel of the KINGDOM. And from there the people receiving the proclamation , then decide if they will believe it or not. And if they do believe in their heart, they will (confess) call upon the name of the Lord towards salvation. Take one part out of order in this progression and you will see some skewing from the originally intended result of the Most High King.

What some refer to as the fivefold ministry (the apostle, prophet, pastor, teacher, and evangelist) should operate from the KINGDOM perspective. If this is not happening, then we see a lot of abuse of these functions in the body of Christ. I believe prophets are inspired preachers or proclaimers. They give direction from a global KINGDOM perspective. Prophets announce but their scope might be beyond even the KINGDOM gospel while they express the wisdom, will, and mind of the Most High. But I believe it is the apostles and evangelists who are called to be the heralds of the KINGDOM of God.

We just mentioned that to preach you must be sent by Christ the King. Well interesting enough, the word "apostle" means sent one. So apostles are sent ones or KINGDOM ambassadors to herald the good news and proclamations of the KINGDOM of God usually to a region or territory. Apostles are high level territorial strategic KINGDOM builders. And evangelist which means carriers of glad tidings and good news (gospel), their proclamation of the good news is more on a personal and congregational level. The pastors who are shepherds, will stick close to the sheep to lead and counsel them in the ways of the KINGDOM. And the teacher will teach the things of the KINGDOM from the Word of God and help mature people in the ways of the KINGDOM. Every function or position, the Most High, is calling people to align with the KINGDOM of God for the express purpose of the KINGDOM.

The scriptures encourage all to do the work of an evangelist but not all are evangelists. Some have been sent and trained in these areas and are more powerful and effective in their KINGDOM proclaiming endeavors. It is like a telemarketer who is just cold calling to get sales versus someone who has been assigned to a particular region or group of people and has a list of leads who are more ready to buy. In whatever KINGDOM area you are called to, make sure you are sent to do what you are doing.

The Gospel of the KINGDOM

From that time Jesus began to preach, and to say, **_Repent: for the KINGDOM of heaven is at hand._** *(Matthew 4:17)*

We know the "who" of the gospel of the KINGDOM is the Lord Jesus Christ (Yeshua). But some might not know what is the good news or the message of the KINGDOM. It seems where some like to complicate things a bit, in the scriptures the proclaiming of the good news was very simple. It all comes down to simply, "Repent for the KINGDOM of heaven is at hand". The announcement is that the KINGDOM is here and at hand and the response to this announcement is to repent.

When John the Baptist came on the scene, what did he preach? "Repent for the KINGDOM of heaven is at hand". When Christ came back from the wilderness after being baptized by John the Baptist, what did he preach? "Repent for the KINGDOM of heaven is at hand". When Christ sent the twelve apostles to go two by two, what did they preach? "The KINGDOM is at hand". And when Christ appointed seventy disciples to go and preach, what did they preach? "The KINGDOM of God is come nigh unto you." The proclamation was clear and concise. The good news was that the KINGDOM of God was near and at hand. This in simplest form is the gospel of the KINGDOM we should convey.

Repentance as the Response

The message of "Repent for the KINGDOM is at hand" is the central theme of the whole bible from the Garden of Eden to the book of Revelation. The KINGDOM (domain of a King) of the Most High has always been the goal and the prize that has been promised through covenant and obedience. But the response of this proclamation and message is to REPENT and align with the ways of the Most High. You want to see the KINGDOM? Repent. You want to enter the KINGDOM of the Most High? Repent. You want to inherit and possess the KINGDOM of heaven and manifest it in the earth? You have to repent.

Repentance and water baptism is the initiation into the KINGDOM of God. That is why water baptism is known as the baptism of repentance. This is key because I believe what we are dealing with today, is that many are not preaching the KINGDOM, nor calling people to repentance nor do many know what the true meaning of repentance is.

This is what is seen in mainstream Christendom. The minister is talking about the sacrifice of Christ and how the blood of Christ has forgiven us of our sins so you can go to heaven when you die. I want to note. I believe this to be true and that it needs to be communicated to people. But this view only paints Christ as a savior but we need to see Christ also as Lord and King. And when we paint him as Lord , then we know the Lord wants all of us and our obedience, And therefore our Lord requires repentance. When Christ is portrayed as King, then that brings the implication that there is a KINGDOM in the mix of this equation.

So then people need to know that heaven is not the end game goal but that a KINGDOM is at play where Christ, right now while you are living, wants to be the King over you, in you, and through you. And for this chain reaction to start in your life, you must repent. Hence, what is the real meaning of repent?

Some think repentance is just saying "God, I am sorry for what I have done" or admitting, "Lord I am a sinner". With this mindset, you have many every day trust in the blood of the Lamb to blot out their sins BUT they have no mind to change. They just keep on going and believing that the blood of the Lamb will cover them. Repentance is more than that. Repentance means to change your mind and thinking or to turn from something to return back to another thing. True repentance comes with the caveat that something must change at my heart, mind, and actions level. Apostle Paul iterated that people who do certain things will not inherit the KINGDOM of God. This shows that the intent of the word of the KINGDOM is to have you turn to the Lord so you can be transformed in his same image. True repentance opens a portal for you to enter the KINGDOM of God.

At Hand Then & Here Right Now

*From that time Jesus began to preach, and to say, Repent: for the KINGDOM of heaven is **at hand.** (Matthew 4:17)*

Repentance is the command that deserves a response when it comes to the gospel of the KINGDOM. But in this section I want to draw attention and highlight the "when" of the simple gospel of the KINGDOM message, which is "at hand". The phrase "at hand" is actually one Greek word "engizo". It means the time is drawing near and that the thing that is being referred to is closely imminent. John the Baptist, the Lord Jesus Christ (Yeshua), and his disciples declared that the KINGDOM of God and heaven was at hand. This was after all the prophetic declarations from the beginning until that time. They understood that they were living in the time and the generation of the fulfillment of commencement of the KINGDOM of God. They knew that Christ was the Messiah and through his name the KINGDOM Age would be ushered in.

There are some that are teaching and waiting that one day soon Christ will crack the sky and establish the KINGDOM then but this was not the understanding of those who heard the proclamation of Christ and his disciples. The KINGDOM was "at hand" to them meaning that it was as close to them as their hands were to their bodies. Back then in that time, the KINGDOM gospel was that the KINGDOM was at hand but now since Christ is the fulfillment, our gospel message should be "Repent for the KINGDOM of God is HERE".

As ambassadors of the gospel of the KINGDOM, you must understand that the KINGDOM of God is here and in operation right now. You must understand that Christ through the cross, resurrection and ascension bruised the head (KINGDOM) of the enemy and spoiled all the principalities and powers. There must be an understanding that in Acts chapter 2 on the day of Pentecost that Apostle Peter declared that this is that which the Prophet Joel prophesied in Joel 2. Christ is sitting on the right hand of the Father and the KINGDOM is in his hands and he is in control. And now if we abide in Christ, we walk in the same KINGDOM authority and we can fully declare and proclaim (preach) with full volume and on the mountain top, "Repent for the KINGDOM of God is here right now. It was "at hand" then, but it is here, right now. We are in the KINGDOM Age right now. The living Christ reigns on the THRONE!!!!

Fully Preaching the Gospel of the KINGDOM

And Jesus went about all the cities and villages, teaching in their synagogues, and **preaching the gospel of the KINGDOM**, *and* **healing every sickness and every disease** *among the people. (Matt. 9:35)*

*And they went forth, and **preached every where**, the Lord working with them, and **confirming the word with signs following**. Amen. (Mark 16:20)*

The KINGDOM of God is now and it is one that operates not only in word and deed BUT in power. The gospel of the KINGDOM brought signs and wonders on the scene back then in Christ's time and it does the same even now. For our God is not a God of respect of person and he honors his Word. Christ is the same yesterday, today, and forever more. And the same Christ and his message that was filled with power two millennia ago, produces the same miraculous works now.

There are some who call themselves cessationists who believe that the gifts of the Spirit of God are no longer in operation. They believe that there are no more apostles and prophets in these modern times. They believe it all died out in the bible times. And I get it because some people are like I don't see the power of God in operation so they logically try to make up theories on why the KINGDOM power of God is not manifesting in their lives. But the key is to look at which seed you are planting to get the fruit that you are harvesting.

The power is in the message. And that message must be a KINGDOM aligned message and you as a preacher must be one who is called and sent. Apostle Paul understood that there was a link to the demonstration of power and the gospel of the KINGDOM. This is why he declared in Romans 1:16 that he was not ashamed of the gospel of Christ because within the gospel of the KINGDOM itself is the "power of God" unto salvation. Christ in Matthew 6 at the end of what we call the Lord's prayer iterated that "thine is the KINGDOM, the power, and glory for ever". The KINGDOM of the Most High cannot exist without the partnership of the power of God and the glory of God. So if we are not experiencing the power and glory of the Most High in our lives, then we need to check what we are proclaiming and preaching. Are we preaching "another gospel"?

*Through mighty signs and wonders, by the power of the Spirit of God; so that from Jerusalem, and round about unto Illyricum, **I have fully preached the gospel of Christ**. (Romans 15:19)*

If we are not seeing signs and wonders as a sign of what we are preaching and proclaiming, then we are not fully preaching the gospel of the KINGDOM. There is a pattern since Christ came on the scene. He preaches the gospel of the KINGDOM and signs and wonders follow. The twelve disciples preached the gospel of the KINGDOM, and guess what? Signs and wonders and the power of God came on the scene. Then you have Apostle Paul who preached the gospel of the KINGDOM and also suggested if the power of God is not operating then he was not fully doing what he was commissioned to do.

The power of God along with signs and wonders is a byproduct of preaching the good news of the KINGDOM of God. I am so passionate about this because it is part of my mandate on the earth to teach people to fully preach the gospel of the KINGDOM and how to demonstrate the power of God. Since then, I have seen the Most High do marvelous things at the preaching of the gospel. I have seen the sick healed, the blind see, the glory of God manifest in amazing ways and people's lives transformed which is the biggest miracle of them all. The highest King of the KINGDOM of the Most High is calling us as KINGDOM believers and ambassadors to fully preach the gospel of Christ with signs and wonders following.

The Good News (Beatitudes)

Matthew 2:2-12

- **2** And he opened his mouth, and taught them, saying,
- **3** Blessed are **the poor in spirit**: for theirs is **the KINGDOM of heaven**.

- **4** Blessed are **they that mourn**: for they **shall be comforted**.
- **5** Blessed are **the meek**: for they shall **inherit the earth**.
- **6** Blessed are they which do **hunger and thirst after righteousness**: for they shall **be filled**.
- **7** Blessed are **the merciful**: for they shall **obtain mercy**.
- **8** Blessed are the **pure in heart**: for they **shall see God**.
- **9** Blessed are **the peacemakers**: for they shall be **called the children of God**.
- **10** Blessed are **they which are persecuted** for righteousness' sake: for theirs is the **KINGDOM of heaven**.
- **11** Blessed are ye, when men **shall revile you**, and persecute you, and shall **say all manner of evil against you falsely,** for my sake.
- **12** Rejoice, and be exceeding glad: for **great is your reward** in heaven

Simply put the good news of the KINGDOM was announced in the Beatitudes which was the beginning of the Sermon on the Mount. Christ proclaimed that people who did certain things were blessed or happy because they would receive certain rewards. The blessing or happiness was always connected to the KINGDOM of the Most High. Those who complied to certain criteria for the KINGDOM, would experience specific things surrounding the KINGDOM. They would be called the children of God. they would obtain mercy and see God. The KINGDOM of heaven would be theirs. They would experience comfort and be filled. Also, Christ let them know that they would inherit the earth and great would be their reward. Christ was declaring the rewards and good news of the KINGDOM in the Beatitudes. When he started the Sermon of the Mount, he began with the good news of the KINGDOM as the main topic.

The Gospel & the KINGDOM Anointing

*17 And there was delivered unto him the book of the prophet Esaias(Isaiah). And when he had opened the book, he found the place where it was written, **18** The Spirit of the Lord is upon me, because **he hath anointed me to preach the gospel** to the poor; he hath sent me to **heal the brokenhearted**, to preach **deliverance to the captives**, and **recovering of sight to the blind**, to **set at liberty them that are bruised**, 19 To preach the **acceptable year of the Lord.** (Luke 4:17-19)*

Did you know that the gospel of the KINGDOM comes along with an anointing? And where this KINGDOM anointing is, the yoke of bondage from the enemy has to be destroyed. In the aforementioned scriptures, we see Christ walking into a synagogue and reading out of the book of Isaiah. This was his custom that he would do when he went into the synagogue and temple. And when he finished reading it, he would close the book and let them know that today in their ears that this scripture was fulfilled. They would all be in amazement because they knew that he was declaring himself as Christ but not only that, he was declaring himself that he was the King that would bring the KINGDOM of God on the scene.

What he read when he was reading out of the book was so powerful and enlightening because Christ conveyed to them that he was sent and anointed to preach the gospel of the KINGDOM. When you are sent from the throne room of heaven and called to do this thing, there is a KINGDOM anointing that falls upon your life because what is on Christ rests on your life as a KINGDOM ambassador. I believe these verses outline the KINGDOM anointing that should rest on those who are ambassadors and witnesses for the KINGDOM of God.

The following are the components of the KINGDOM Anointing:

- The power to preach the gospel of the KINGDOM

- The power to heal the brokenhearted
- The power to bring deliverance to those who are in captivity
- The power to recover the sight of the blind
- The power to set those in liberty who are bruised
- To power to preach and declare the acceptable year of the Lord (judgment)

The power and anointing is in the appointed vessel and the message. My intent is to speak of this at a high level as this eventually will be contained in a book entitled "KINGDOM Anointing". The KINGDOM anointing is versatile to address physical and mental healing, blindness, and deliverance from oppression of the enemy.

*17 And **these signs shall follow them that believe**; In my name shall they cast out devils; they shall speak with new tongues; 18 They shall take up serpents; and if they drink any deadly thing, it shall not hurt them; they shall lay hands on the sick, and they shall recover. (Mark 16:17-18)*

The list mentioned is in no way exhaustive and full because the power of God can do all things. Mark 16, another set of scriptures align to the KINGDOM anointing . This anointing carried by us who are believers means that we can cast out devils, not be harmed by deadly drink or serpent poisonous bites, and we can lay hands on the sick and they will recover. In the KINGDOM of the Most High, all things are impossible and nothing is too hard for him.

There is probably someone who questioned about the scripture in Luke chapter 4 that Christ was reading about himself and they ask, "Isn't this just about the anointing that Christ operated in? I will answer this with a resounding 'NO". In Mark 16, it describes what the believers in Christ will do. So this shows that we are called to walk in power and KINGDOM authority. And I don't see any time limits on this scripture. But also, I want to introduce that Christ is the head and we are the body. And what is on the head also, indeed functions on the body.

*It is like the **precious ointment upon the head**, that ran down upon the beard, even Aaron's beard: that **went down to the skirts of his garments**; (Psalms 133:2)*

As mentioned in Psalms 133:2, when in context of what happens when the brethren are in unity and alignment, it lets us know that the anointing (ointment) that is on the head , will then flow to the beard. And it doesn't stop there. It continues from the beard to flow to the skirts of the priest garment as well. The anointing is not just for the head, but it is for the body as well. As Christ is in this present world and age, so are we. Let's press into the KINGDOM of the Most High and proclaim his KINGDOM and walk in his KINGDOM anointing.

What The Enemy Is After

*18 Hear ye therefore the parable of the sower. 19 **When any one heareth the word of the KINGDOM**, and understandeth it not, **then cometh the wicked one**, and catcheth away that which was sown in his heart. This is he which received seed by the way side. 20 But he that received the seed into stony places, the same is he that heareth the word, and anon with joy receiveth it; 21 Yet hath he not root in himself, but dureth for a while: for when tribulation or persecution ariseth because of the word, by and by he is offended. 22 He also that received seed among the thorns is he that heareth the word; and the care of this world, and the deceitfulness of riches, choke the word, and he becometh unfruitful. 23 But he that received seed into the good ground is he that heareth the word, and understandeth it; which also beareth fruit, and bringeth forth, some an hundredfold, some sixty, some thirty. (Matthew 13:18-23)*

So in the chapter of Matthew 13, we have what is known as the parable of the sower. The part featured is actually the interpretation of what Christ said in parable format after the disciples asked for more clarification. I believe the focus is not only on the sower but also on the seed and where you sow the seed. I have heard many messages on this text of scripture and what the "seed" represents. But we don't have to guess or try to conjure up what the seed represents because Christ clearly told us what the seed represented. Per verse 19, The seed represents the "word of the KINGDOM". It is not just any type of word. It is not the word about faith, joy, peace, and whatever else you can think of. But it is a specified word. It is the word of the KINGDOM. It is the gospel of the KINGDOM.

There are many places I can go with these scriptures but what I want to draw focus on is that this seed which represents the gospel of the KINGDOM is so powerful that if it is planted in the right soil and received in the right way, then it will produce great dividends and a great harvest. It is so potent and magnificent that the enemy is coming immediately to kill, steal, and destroy the word of the KINGDOM. This seed of the gospel of the KINGDOM is not a seed that is meant to operate in a surface area type of environment. But the Most High engineered it that it only grows when it is planted deep in the recesses of your heart and through time and patience and tribulation is able to grow into something beautiful with much fruit.

I am not saying that the enemy is not concerned about other things. But most definitely it is the word of the KINGDOM (the gospel of the KINGDOM) that is so high of a priority that he stops everything he is doing to come immediately to uproot that seed of the gospel of the KINGDOM. The KINGDOM of God is designed to be within you and so the enemy comes right away to grab this KINGDOM word before it can take root deep inside. It is the gospel and the good news of the KINGDOM that is a threat to the enemy and his so-called KINGDOM. This word of the KINGDOM is what the enemy is after.

KINGDOM Discipleship

18 Jesus came up and said to them, "All authority (all power of absolute rule) in heaven and on earth has been given to Me. 19 **Go therefore and make disciples** *of all the nations [help the people to learn of Me, believe in Me, and obey My words], baptizing them in the name of the Father and of the Son and of the Holy Spirit, 20 teaching them to observe everything that I have commanded you; (Matthew 28:18-20 AMP)*

At the end of chapter 28 of Matthew before Christ ascends to the Father, Christ gives his disciples what some call the "Great Commission". Here Christ is commanding them to go into all the world and preach the gospel of the KINGDOM. What for? To make disciples. He did not tell them to make converts or go get church members but he told them to make disciples. Why is this important? It is important because discipleship is the fruit of the gospel of the KINGDOM.

Some experiences for some is that they went to a gathering or a church service and a message about Christ was preached. They preached Christ as a savior and talked about forgiveness of sins and about God's grace. And after that, they had people come to repeat words of a sinner's prayer from their mental and not from their heart and now everything is all good from their eyes. The KINGDOM of God was not proclaimed. Christ was only advertised as a savior and not as Lord and King and the mindset for some is God understands my weaknesses and sin and so I can keep on doing what I was doing before because the grace of God got me covered. So they are just converts and church members but not striving to be disciples of Christ.

When the true KINGDOM gospel is preached and goes into our hearts, it produces a KINGDOM fold harvest and transformation in our lives. I am not knocking being a church member but the real question is, are you a KINGDOM disciple of Christ? You might say how do you know? One indicator would be that of the main goals of your life is to be conformed to the image of Christ and be like him. As the Amplified version of Matthew 28 points out, are we looking to *learn of Christ, believe in Christ and obey the Words of Christ?*

The fruit of the KINGDOM of God in your life is for you to be like Christ. This is done by being a disciple of Christ. Being a disciple of Christ means that Christ is your Master and King and you are willing to come up from under the yoke of bondage of the enemy to take on the yoke of Christ to learn of him. A disciple of Christ seeks to have an intimate relationship with Christ and also look for other mature leaders in the KINGDOM of God to learn under. True disciples of Christ and his KINGDOM bear the fruit of the KINGDOM which is the righteousness and love of Christ.

If you want to know if the gospel of the KINGDOM has taken root in your heart, then take an inventory within and see if you desire change and transformation before anything else. Are you willing to take up your own cross and die daily and follow him? This is the cry and yearning in the heart of a KINGDOM disciple. The gospel of the KINGDOM is such a powerful seed that it can be planted and create KINGDOM disciples who mature to become KINGDOM ambassadors who plant seeds to grow more KINGDOM disciples. The KINGDOM disciple allows Christ to reign on the throne of their hearts. We must have the burning seed of the gospel of the KINGDOM in us to boldly cry out loud and spare not with the words, "Repent, for the KINGDOM of God is here and available now". Come and get it. Come now to see and enter the KINGDOM of the Most High God.

Chapter 7 : Seek The KINGDOM First

*But seek ye **first the KINGDOM of God**, and his righteousness; and all these things shall be added unto you. (Matthew 6:33)*

In our Heavenly Father's eyes, everything is about his KINGDOM. It is at the heart of the intention of all he does. The good news (gospel) that should be published in all the world is about the KINGDOM of God. Christ the King would tell his disciples that he would not say or do anything unless he first saw his Father do the same thing. Christ is the express image of the Father and so we have to pay very close attention to his words that are spirit and life. The KINGDOM of God was Christ's number one topic when he was here on the earth. And not only was it his number one topic, it was also his number one priority for us to walk in. Hence, the scripture above, which in some bibles would be red letters as the words of Christ, iterates that we are to seek the KINGDOM of God first.

The KINGDOM of God is the rule of Father and Son in you, over you, and through you with the intent that they be all in all. The heart of the Father for us is to seek the KINGDOM with all of our heart. He did not tell us to seek first finances and riches. He did not tell us to seek what he can bless us with first. Nor did he tell us to seek fame and notoriety first. Very interesting, we were not told to seek our basic needs of food, water, and clothing first. He actually told us not to think or worry about those things because he already knows what we need. And if we seek the KINGDOM of God first, the rest will be added. What can be more important than food and clothes? The answer is simple. In Christ Jesus' mind, the KINGDOM of God is the most important thing we can ever pursue. We are to seek the KINGDOM of God first.

Righteousness Also

*For the **KINGDOM of God** is not meat and drink; but **righteousness**, and peace, and joy in the Holy Ghost.(Romans 14:17)*

Romans 14:17 lets the reader know that righteousness is an aspect of the KINGDOM of God along with peace and joy in the Holy Ghost. It is not about what you eat or drink but about the trio of righteousness, peace, and joy. If you are not walking in peace or joy, you are not experiencing the KINGDOM of God in your life at that moment. This is a clear indicator. But let's put more emphasis on righteousness. Righteousness is key because along with Christ saying to seek first the KINGDOM, he also includes righteousness. We are to seek first the KINGDOM and righteousness. We just saw that righteousness is a facet of the KINGDOM but it must be so important that Christ had to elevate and highlight righteousness itself along with the KINGDOM. This implies in Christ's eyes, before peace and joy, righteousness has more weight. So if I may, I believe Christ was saying to us and his disciples that they need to seek the KINGDOM first and the first aspect of the KINGDOM you need to seek first is his righteousness.

The question someone might ponder is what is righteousness. Someone might answer that it is being in right standing with God. Another might echo that it is being holy and doing good works. Someone else might interject that it is being pious, pure in heart, and reaching some type of marker in God's eyes. But as you might have already seen, I like to go to the Greek for better context and definition. Righteousness here is the Greek word "dikaiosyne" which means in a broad sense a person being in a state that is acceptable and approved of God. It continues that this righteousness is having the character or quality of being right or just.

So the perspective of righteousness is always from the eyes of the Most High and King that is why it says "his righteousness". It is what the King deems as acceptable to cause you to have right standing before him. And this righteousness is not just an outward working but more importantly, it is the character and inward state within a person that God is looking at. Man might judge that something is righteous from an outward perspective but God looks at the heart and their inward parts. It is righteousness that grants you access to the Most High and his KINGDOM. Righteousness is not being perfect but it is aligning yourself to be accepted by him.

In righteousness, there are two points there. It is a mixture of who you are and what is the testimony (records) of your works. This is why Christ is so pivotal to us being righteous before the Father. It is because of the sacrifice of Christ that we have his blood and his Spirit. We need both. We need the Holy Spirit to birth us again into his KINGDOM and change who we are in the sight of the Father. But we also need the blood of the Lamb to blot out the record and testimony of our past and our present that was against us. It is through the blood of the Lamb and being a new creation that we gain access and have right standing in the KINGDOM of the Most High. We are to seek first the KINGDOM but know that also means we need to seek first the righteousness of God. Righteousness goes hand in hand with the KINGDOM of God and the scepter of the KINGDOM of God is one of righteousness.

Believe & Repent

And saying, The time is fulfilled, and the KINGDOM of God is at hand: **repent** *ye, and* **believe the gospel***. (Mark 1:15)*

Before in other gospels like that of Matthew, we have seen one version of this previous scripture about the KINGDOM of God being at hand. But in the book of Mark it adds that the time has been fulfilled and you need to repent and believe the good news of the KINGDOM. In the previous paragraph, I mentioned the importance of the blood of the Lamb and the Holy Spirit. But I wanted to highlight here that if you want to kick start the KINGDOM of the Most High in your life to seek the KINGDOM first, you must first believe the gospel of the KINGDOM and then follow it up by repentance.

There is no KINGDOM explosion in your life without first hearing the good news of the KINGDOM and from that, then yielding to the Lord through repentance. To believe the gospel is to have faith because you have been persuaded by the good news so much that you had to stop going in the direction you were going in your life and literally turn to the Lord. This is what repentance is , changing your direction. It is changing from doing it your way. It is good to just say I'm sorry but repentance is allowing real change to happen in your life.

The example that I have pictured in my mind is that of a married couple where the husband is an abusive man. Unfortunately, many of us have seen this situation a number of times where a man is constantly beating and putting his hands on his wife. And from what I can tell there are some abusive men who continually go through a cycle of hitting their wives, and then even with tears tell their wives that they are sorry, and then continue to do the same things over and over again. This is a picture of someone who has said I am sorry but has not done true repentance.

Sometimes this is how we treat our Heavenly Father where we are just saying sorry but we are not doing true repentance. We can look real convincing with our tears and kneeling down but are our hearts truly sincere? In Hebrews 12:17, there is an example with Esau where he sought repentance with tears before the Most High and found no repentance. Why? Because it is not about what you are saying in a moment of saying I am sorry but it is what you do after that moment of saying you are sorry. Repent means again to change your mind. Repentance comes with change.

So how do we really know that you believe the good news of the KINGDOM? How do we know you are truly walking in faith and in the persuasion of what you heard? How do we truly know that the word and seed of the KINGDOM was planted deep in your heart? We know because through the trials, tribulation, and temptations, you were able to change and continue to mature in the things of the Most High. To begin to seek first the KINGDOM and his righteousness we must truly believe in our heart and repent with a sign of change.

Invisible KINGDOM

For by him were all things created, that are in heaven, and that are in earth, **visible and invisible***, whether they be thrones, or dominions, or principalities, or powers: all things were created by him, and for him: (Colossians 1:16)*

A caveat we must consider in trying to seek the KINGDOM first is that a great majority of the KINGDOM of the Most High is invisible to the natural eyes of most of mankind. In Colossians 1:16, we read that if we look at all creation, there are parts of heaven and earth and there are some parts that are visible and invisible. And when we are talking about the reigning components of the KINGDOM such as thrones, dominions, principalities, powers, and the throne of the Most High, they are invisible. In other words, if you don't have the right eyes, then the KINGDOM of the Most High is invisible to you.

When Adam and Eve were first formed, they had the ability to see the heavenly realms and interact with the earthly realm at the same time. They were able to hear and see the King as well. They had access to the KINGDOM but then the fall happened and another set of eyes and perspective came on the scene. Some might say Christ came so now we can go to heaven when we die but I say not so. This is like going to an ice cream shop and ordering a banana split and just eating a tip of the banana and throwing away the rest of the banana, the ice cream, whip cream, cherry and syrup. There is so much more to the package of the KINGDOM of the Most High.

The purpose of Christ was to bring us back to the state of Eden and beyond. Christ came to do a full redemption and restoration. He came to bring us to another level of access and awareness. He wanted to allow us to be born again so now we can SEE the KINGDOM once again. He wanted to make us a new creation so we can fully enjoy the whole of creation. That is why he is telling us to SEEK, whose base word is "see", the KINGDOM so we can "see" that which was previously invisible to us. And being born again, we can see those dimensions and the realms of the KINGDOM right now. Not only see it, but enter into it as well. And not to stop there but literally operate and possess the things of the KINGDOM. It is all available to us now.

*For the **invisible things of him** from the creation of the world are clearly seen, being understood by the things that are made, even his eternal power and Godhead; so that they are **without excuse**: (Romans 1:20)*

Above is another scripture that shows that some aspects of creation were invisible while living in the earth realm and looking through our natural eyes. But the beautiful part is that God in his wisdom allowed some things from the invisible realm to be paralleled in the visible earth realm so we can understand on some level heavenly things and long for the invisible. And it is because of this, even if we are in our fallen state and can only see through the natural eyes, we are without excuse because he left some breadcrumbs behind to help us find our way back home. But now we have Christ our Messiah and King who is the light of the world who has now made the invisible KINGDOM visible for us to see.

Not of this World

Not only is the KINGDOM of God without being born again, invisible, but it is not of this world. It is above you and it is within you. That is a paradox for you. How can both exist and be true? Because the things and thoughts of the Most High are higher than our thoughts and ways and some things can not be reasoned out by intelligence but must be spiritually discerned. You have to grab it by faith.

> **20** *And when he was demanded of the Pharisees, when the KINGDOM of God should come, he answered them and said,* **The KINGDOM of God cometh not with observation: 21** *Neither shall they say,* **Lo here! or, lo there! for, behold, the KINGDOM of God is within you**. *(Luke 17:20-21)*

In Luke 17, the Pharisees demanded of Christ to tell them when the KINGDOM would come and in another place the disciples thought that the KINGDOM would be some military takeover in the earthly realm. The Jews, even today, are looking for some type of earthly military leader to come on the scene to be the Messiah. But Christ let them know that the KINGDOM of God is not with observation with your visible physical eyes. You will not be able to say it is here or there. You will not be able to say go to Mt. Zion or Mt. Sinai and the KINGDOM be there. But the KINGDOM of God is within you. The KINGDOM of God is in the realm of spirit and truth. God is a spirit and you must find the KINGDOM in the realm of spirit of truth for this is where the KINGDOM of God resides.

*Yet a little while, and **the world seeth me no more; but ye see me**: because I live, ye shall live also. (John 14:19)*

In John 14:19, Christ lets the disciples know that there is a possibility for those of the world not to see him, but they who are no longer of this world, they would be able to see him. I have been in a room with others and I see angels but others don't see those angels. Because they don't see the angels, does that mean the angels don't exist? No, it means that at that moment their spiritual eyes were not in tune to see the angels. The realm of the KINGDOM to some is invisible and not of this world but to those who hunger after the KINGDOM to seek , the Most High will open their eyes and grant them access. There is a protocol if you begin to seek first the KINGDOM of God so that which is invisible , he will make visible to you. And that which is not of this world, he will bring you to and make available to you.

Where the King Is

*2 In my Father's house are many mansions: if it were not so, I would have told you. I go to prepare a place for you. 3 And if I go and **prepare a place for you**, I will come again, and receive you unto myself; **that where I am, there ye may be also**. (John 14:2-3)*

Just like the Pharisees, some might want to know when the KINGDOM of God is? The KINGDOM of God is NOW. And just like the disciples who asked for Christ to show them the Father and the KINGDOM. The KINGDOM is not one physical place but in the Father's house and KINGDOM there are many rooms. It is vast and bigger than just the heavens and just the earth. It is ever increasing and don't forever think that all creation has stopped for there are many galaxies. There is no limit to our God and King.

So someone might ask where is the KINGDOM of God? Christ in one place of scripture lets you know it is within you. But that is one aspect of its location. I believe that he pointed to the place where he wants you to begin to seek first the KINGDOM. It is in you. Because Colossians 1 lets us know that the mystery that has been hidden all this time that is now being revealed is that Christ is in you and he is your hope of glory. Christ lives in you and he is your King in this KINGDOM.

In John 14:3, the emphasis is not so much on the place of the KINGDOM, but more on the who. It expresses that the goal is not a place but for you to be where he is. That is the main goal for you to be where the King is. So if I had to answer where the KINGDOM is? I give you the answer the Holy Spirit told me. If you need a King for there to be a KINGDOM, then the KINGDOM begins where the King is. If you are seeking the KINGDOM of God first, then you must seek where the King is. Because where he is, is where his KINGDOM is. Christ is sitting at the right hand of the Father in heaven but also in his omnipresence is dwelling within you. Hence, the KINGDOM of God is within you.

The KINGDOM is not only about dominion and image but it is about relationships. Christ came to reconcile us back to the Father in heaven. It is about the Kings, the Father and the Son. Later in John 14, Christ lets us know that it is possible for the world not to see him but we see him. Why? Because it is about our relationship with the Father and Son. In John 17:3, true eternal life was defined as to know the Father and Son. The KINGDOM is where the King is.

*21 He that hath my commandments, and keepeth them, he it is that loveth me: and he that loveth me shall be loved of my Father, and I will love him, and **will manifest myself to him**. 22 Judas saith unto him, not Iscariot, Lord, **how is it that thou wilt manifest thyself unto us, and not unto the world?** 23 Jesus answered and said unto him, If a man love me, he will keep my words: and my Father will love him, and **we will come unto him, and make our abode with***

him. (John 14:21)

There might be an objection concerning John 14:3 that this scripture is talking about the second coming of Christ. But I beg to differ. Many want to see it that way because they have more of an escapist mindset of let's leave the earth and get to heaven. But the saga of the KINGDOM of God is a love story between us and the Father and Son so we can manifest the KINGDOM of heaven on earth. Later in chapter 14 of John, Christ talks about the ability of seeing him and how the world would be able to see him while we are still on the earth. It then continues in verse 21 to show if we obey his commandments and keep them, then we will be loved by the Father and Christ will "manifest" himself to us. (This is a key verse. You want to know what the commandments of Jesus are, then read Matthew chapters 5-7 which is the constitution of the KINGDOM of God.)

"Manifest" means to reveal that which is invisible and make it visible. Christ to those who qualify while they are the earth, he will manifest himself to them. Judas was so intrigued by this, he asked, "how is it that you will manifest yourself to us and not the rest of the world?" Christ then goes another step and said not only will he manifest himself to us but the Father and him will come and make their abode with us. In other words, they will give us access to their abode and KINGDOM.

I know some might not agree or like what I am about to say here. But some are waiting for a rapture where he takes us all at one time but they are missing the rapture of love where Christ through our obedience comes and reveals his KINGDOM to us individually. This is the rapture of the KINGDOM that can happen within you and then make room for you to ascend to other realms of his KINGDOM. I hope this is not blowing the minds of some but it is my intention to bring you to the KINGDOM perspective and know there is more to the KINGDOM of the Most High. And we are being called to pursue it. The whole of creation is groaning for the manifestations of the Sons of God in the earth and if we limit ourselves with a limited perspective, then we will not be the manifested Sons of God in the earth. But this starts with us seeking where the King is so we can be like him.

Progression of the KINGDOM: See, Enter, Inherit, Enlarge

*3 Jesus answered and said unto him, Verily, verily, I say unto thee, Except a man be born again, he cannot **see the KINGDOM of God**. 4 Nicodemus saith unto him, How can a man be born when he is old? can he enter the second time into his mother's womb, and be born? 5 Jesus answered, Verily, verily, I say unto thee, Except a man be born of water and of the Spirit, he cannot **enter into the KINGDOM of God**.*

The KINGDOM of God is like a seed that is planted and it becomes one of the biggest trees where the fowls of the air can lodge in them. It starts at one point as a seed, then spouts with its first blade and from there branches to eventually fruit. There is a progression to the KINGDOM of God. The KINGDOM of God is invisible and you have to get to the place where you can see it. When you see it, then you can enter it. When you enter it, then you can inherit and possess it. And once it is in your possession and you know the workings of it, then you must then be fruitful and multiply it . The KINGDOM cannot stay at a stand still. It must be increased and enlarged. Therefore the progression of the KINGDOM of God is for you to see it, enter it, inherit (possess) it, and enlarge it.

See (Awareness)

The KINGDOM of God is not obvious to the natural eye. It is not something that can be understood by pure logic and a high intellectual prowess. The Most High even wants you to experience the KINGDOM with all your spiritual senses and not just hearing. He wants you to see the KINGDOM. He wants you to taste the KINGDOM and see that it is good. He wants you to hear the things of the KINGDOM because faith comes by hearing. But even more on that, he wants you to see the KINGDOM which is why he made it possible for you to be born again. By being born again, you gain awareness with all your spiritual senses to be able to see.

If any man be in Christ , he is a new creation. You are now alive in your inner man and can see and experience things that you could not experience before. And this should be your expectation to operate in this new found sight to experience the Heavenly Father in the way that Adam and Eve experienced him in the garden. After the fall, there was a need for sight so you can operate in the KINGDOM that the Father had in store for us.

The reason to be born again is twofold. First we needed to regain the "image" of the Son and bloodline to be able to rule and have dominion as a birthright. But second, sight has to be regained. If we can only hear but cannot see, we are not at our full strength. If God is a spirit and the things concerning him are spiritual, then we need to see and discern things spiritually to really be effective as the kings and priests that he has ordained us to be. How do you become what you are supposed to be? By seeing.

One spiritual law based out of 2 Corinthians 3:18, is that we become what we see. The next chapter of 2 Corinthians then goes on to show that we have the treasure of Christ within us, the earthen vessel, and now we can see the glory of God through the "face" of Christ. Christ said he only does what he saw the Father to do. So we need to see Christ and be changed into the same image but also see Christ in his Kingly role so we can imitate that which we have seen to be Kings ourselves. You can't be satisfied with just hearing but your cry within should be I want to see it. The first progression of the KINGDOM of the Most High is to see it.

Enter (Access)

The second aspect of the progression is to transition from seeing to be able to enter in. This is all about access. It is very hard to enter something you can't see. How can you know what direction to go if you cannot see? Someone who is blind will need some type of assistance from someone else who can see. Also, a person might not be blind but there is so much darkness around they can't see. The Holy Spirit is the one who leads you and Christ is the light of the world to disperse the darkness so you can see and enter.

A person can be in a position and be near the location where they want to be but due to blindness or darkness they might not be able to see the intended destination and therefore can't enter it. They might be facing north when they need to be going east. So sight is very important when it comes to the ability to be able to enter something.

I like to use the illustration of the tabernacle and temple in the Old Testament. With the tabernacle, you have the outer court that encircles the tabernacle. In the outer court you have the brazen altar and brazen laver where the sacrifices occur. Then you have the holy place which has the golden candlestick, golden table of showbread, and the golden altar of incense. Then the next area is the holy of holies or the most holy place where you have the golden ark of the covenant with the mercy seat.

In this example, the outer court and the holy place are separated by the door. And the holy place and the most holy place is separated by the veil. Anyone can be in the outer court, but you need to be a priest to go into the holy place and you have to be the high priest to go into the most holy place.

Anyone in the outer court, can see the tabernacle but that does not mean you can enter it. So God wants you to be able as priests in his KINGDOM of priests to enter the tabernacle. And as you mature even more and become like Christ and abide in Christ the high priest, then you can advance and enter further into the most holy place and fellowship with the Father. There is an invitation for you to come and enter the KINGDOM so you come to a place to know the throne room of God and be reconciled to the Father as a mature son in his KINGDOM.

When you are born again of his Spirit, then you are able to see. And faith is the substance of things hoped for and the evidence of things not seen. Now being able to see, you are able to see the substance of the KINGDOM and its evidence. Because faith gives you eyes to see the unseen and invisible. So how do you enter? You press and enter the KINGDOM by believing the promises of the King. You also believe in the power of the blood of the Lamb and you enter in by faith.

*Confirming the souls of the disciples, and exhorting them to **continue in the faith**, and that we must **through much tribulation enter into the KINGDOM of God**. (Acts 14:22)*

You have to continue in faith to enter the KINGDOM of God but I believe another aspect people don't realize is that to enter the KINGDOM comes with the price of tribulation. Romans 5 starting at around verse 3 lets us know that we glory in tribulation. Without tribulation, there is no glory. And glory is the goal because glory is the atmosphere that surrounds the King of glory in the most holy place. To see is one thing but to enter into the deeper and higher aspects of the KINGDOM comes with a price. That is why many are called but few are chosen. Many will be able to go to heaven when they die but not all will be able to enter into and inherit the KINGDOM. This comes through tribulation and frankly not everyone wants to go through that process.

*And he said to them all, If **any man will come after me**, **let him deny himself**, and **take up his cross daily**, and **follow me**. (Luke 9:23)*

The process comes with tribulation and you have to die to yourself to follow Christ and enter the KINGDOM. That is what entering the KINGDOM is all about. It is about following Christ to where he is. The KINGDOM is where the King is. And the price to follow him is to take up your own cross and identify with Christ and deny who you were before with all your dreams and aspirations to follow him as high priest to be in the greater parts of the KINGDOM. To be joint heirs while having a place with him on his throne and being where he is, you have to walk in faith, deny yourself, die to yourself, and press through the tribulation. As you enter the KINGDOM you will experience the revelation of his Word, the fullness of the Holy Spirit and Christ, and the Heavenly Father on another level.

Inherit (Possess)

*Then shall the King say unto them on his right hand, Come, ye blessed of my Father, **inherit the KINGDOM** prepared for you from the foundation of the world: (Matthew 25:34)*

In scripture, there have been occurrences that have already been shared in this book, that shows that you can see the KINGDOM and enter the KINGDOM. But the next phase in the KINGDOM progression is to inherit the KINGDOM. I want you to keep the perspective that the KINGDOM is not far off but the KINGDOM is now. You do not have to wait until you die to inherit the KINGDOM for there is KINGDOM work to do on the earth. An inheritance usually comes when someone dies. Well Christ has died already and tasted death for all men so we can now inherit the KINGDOM.

The Greek word for "inherit" is "kleronomeo" and it means to receive an inheritance that you have a right to that is allotted just for you as a possession. So I like to interchange the word "inherit" with the word "possess" because when you inherit, you now have ownership of your own domain and territory. You are now joint heirs with the King of Kings. You are more than just being a servant in the KINGDOM who can see it and enter it, but now you have reached a level of being a matured son who now can fully possess your portion. This reminds me in Daniel 7 when it talks about the arrival of Christ and that is when the saints can begin to possess (inherit) the KINGDOM.

*He that **overcometh shall inherit all things**; and I will be his God, and **he shall be my son**. (Revelation 21:7)*

How do you get to the place to move from just seeing and entering to inheriting and possessing? You have to overcome. When you become born again, you are at infant level but then you, through the guidance of the Holy Spirit and the tutelage of the seven spirits of God, can come to maturity. This is where the Father can declare over you as he announces you to heaven and earth, "This is my Son in whom I am well pleased. Hear ye him".

In a later chapter of this book, I will point out some of the things that we as manifested Sons in the earth must overcome. We must overcome the enemy, the flesh, the world, and the law of sin and death. At the state of overcoming, then we can inherit all things where all things are possible through Christ. You can begin to walk in another level of authority where your words don't fall to the ground. You are fully conformed to the image of Christ and understand the workings of the KINGDOM of God. You, at this stage will not only know the Son intimately, but also the Father as well. This comes with another level of responsibility.

This stage is one of possession and ownership. You are not only a King under the King of Kings but you are a Lord under the Lord of Lords because being a Lord deals with ownership. Some of you have probably rented properties before and you had a landlord or a lord of that particular land. But when you inherit the KINGDOM, you are a King and Lord who now has an allotted territory and domain that the Most High has given you oversight of. You see things from a heavenly perspective and have an acquaintance with the higher realms of the KINGDOM of God. We are called to see, enter, and inherit the KINGDOM of the Most High.

Enlarge (Increase & Multiply)

*And God blessed them, and God said unto them, Be fruitful, **and multiply, and*** *replenish the earth*, *and subdue it: and* **have dominion** *over the fish of the sea, and over the fowl of the air, and over every living thing that moveth upon the earth. (Genesis 1:28)*

Of the increase of his government and peace there shall be no end, *upon the throne of David, and upon his KINGDOM, to order it, and to establish it with judgment and with justice from henceforth even for ever. (Isaiah 9:7)*

In the Father's heart, it is not enough for his children to possess and inherit the KINGDOM. He wants us to have the same mindset he possesses which is enlargement. Part of my definition for the KINGDOM of the Most High stated in the introduction is that his intention is to be all in all. The goal of the KINGDOM of the Most High is to find the areas of darkness and expand into those territories with the light of the KINGDOM. Our mindset should be to have a KINGDOM outbreak throughout all the earth. I remember when I was younger there was a movie called *Outbreak* where there was an outbreak of a disease of pandemic proportions. And in that movie I remember a scene where they showed a world map where a little red spot represented the spread of the disease and how in a short time the whole world map was red. Oh the Father wants to see the whole earth and his KINGDOM be full of red that represents the blood of Christ at work.

Also, this theme makes me think of two songs I used to listen to back in the day. One song "Bless Me" by Donald Lawrence had verbiage that echoed "Enlarge My Territory". Also, Israel Houghton had a song called "No Limits" where the cry of the song is, "Take the limits off. Enlarge My Territory". It is something about these two songs that always increased a fire and excitement in my spirit because it let me know that there are no limits to the KINGDOM of God. It is steadily advancing and ever enlarging and increasing.

One of the scriptures highlighted at the beginning of this section comes from Genesis 1:28 where we see the Most High calling to mankind is to be fruitful and multiply. The KINGDOM is about an enduring legacy. It is one thing to inherit and be fruitful but he also wants us to multiply what he has placed inside us. We have to move from just thinking about the KINGDOM at an individual level. But we have to let the light of the KINGDOM increase and penetrate at the family level, the community level, the city level, the nation level, and also at an international level. When you inherit, you might be given a little part of the pie. But if you are faithful in the few and little, he will increase you with the many and more.

The KINGDOM in some of Christ's parables, is parallel to agriculture endeavors. The KINGDOM is like a seed that grows into a tree and into a garden. The Most High is looking for expansion and growth. In Isaiah 9:7, we are told that the increase of Christ's government (KINGDOM) will be no end. This implies that the fullness of the KINGDOM will not happen all at once but will be incremental as his KINGDOM Sons rise up, overcome, inherit, and eventually enlarge the KINGDOM. Expansion, enlargement, and increase is the last leg of the progression of the KINGDOM working in our lives.

Protocol of the KINGDOM: Ask, Seek. & Knock

*7 **Ask**, and it **shall be given** you; **seek**, and **ye shall find**; **knock**, and **it shall be opened** unto you: **8** For every one that asketh receiveth; and he that seeketh findeth; and to him that knocketh it shall be opened. (Matthew 7:7-8)*

There are stages to the progression of the KINGDOM being increased in our lives from seeing, to entering, to inheriting, and then enlarging it. But this is not automatic and there are some protocol steps that must happen for you to really begin the journey of seeking the KINGDOM of God and his righteousness first. The KINGDOM is not just going to fall in your lap. It is not just going to appear and say here I am. No, we have to seek it. On some level it is hidden and invisible. That is why one scripture says that it must be pressed into it because it is going to take some intention, hunger, and pursuit on our end.

But before we seek, we must ask first. This asking might go in line with repentance or confession that you believe the good news of the KINGDOM. But if you want it, there has to be a part of you that has to ask. There has to be a cry deep in the recesses of you that says, "God give me the KINGDOM!!!". I don't even say that it is a formal question of , "Father, can I have the KINGDOM?" because we should know it is his will and pleasure to give us the KINGDOM. But he is looking for an act of your will and choice that says Father I want it and I want it all no matter what it takes. And in that asking in faith, we have to receive it in faith. We have to trust that if we asked, then we received it right then. As I like to tell my children, you have to ask. You have to use your words because a closed mouth doesn't get fed.

Because you have asked and received it, does not mean you are fully experiencing the fullness of what you have received. Have you gotten a gift , but it was wrapped up? So you had to tear off the wrapping paper to then find the present. You can see what it is, but that item is now wrapped in plastic and in a box that you might need scissors or some other tool to use to get to the contents. Then you get inside the inner box, and then you have instructions and/or activation codes. Then you might have to assemble it to actually enjoy the present. I use this illustration to show there are some steps involved to actually enjoy the fullness of the KINGDOM.

Also, maybe you are a gamer. And you just got a brand new video game. It is the ultimate game and you can't wait to download it into your game system and get to the highest levels of the game to declare yourself as the overcoming victor who conquered the game. But of course you could not just jump to the last level. You even see that some of the levels are locked waiting for you to beat the preceding levels. Also, the game might come with basic tools and weapons, but now you realize you have to pay the price to get the special weapons that will aid you to reach the end of the game. The quest for the KINGDOM is like this in many ways. It is more simple than just asking and receiving it. You have to seek and go on the quest for the KINGDOM.

You ask in faith. You receive in faith. But you also must seek with faith. How do you seek the KINGDOM? Some of the keys to seek him is through meditation of the Word, prayer, and fasting. Meditation of the Word causes the KINGDOM Word to be written in your hearts and mind. Prayer causes you to ask your heavenly father for the KINGDOM to come and for his will to be done on earth as it is heaven. The other part of prayer causes you to be more intimate with the Holy Spirit and wait in his presence as he guides you in deeper aspects of the KINGDOM. And then fasting helps you to put your body under and afflict your soul to remove the limitations and weights of the flesh to aid you to ascend in the realms of the KINGDOM. The word, prayer and fasting mixed together will bring great results as you seek the KINGDOM. It is a process and takes patience.

When you reach one phase, you can't think that you have arrived because after you have sought in your journey of seeking, you might see there is a door in your way. And that door is locked and you need someone to open that door. If you come to someone's house you don't just stand outdoors and do nothing. Neither is it appropriate for you to go around and find an open window to climb into. The right thing is to knock or ring that doorbell. I love that the bible uses the word "knock" because that aligns with taking the KINGDOM by force violently. When you want someone to open a door and you are excited about coming in, you don't just barely tap that door. No, you knock, as we like to say where I come from, like it's the police.

Knocking insinuates that you see something but can't get in and wish to enter so you can experience what is inside. Also, when I think about knocking which can be powerful and forceful, I believe there has to be a hunger and passion to enter. It is this passion that gets the King's attention to let you in. He wants us to love him with all our heart and mind, but also desires that we love him with all our might and strength (passion). It is your passion and desire that will be the fuel that causes you to enter into new aspects of the KINGDOM. If you knew your child was held captive behind a door, there is no door that you will not knock down. Your passion might be so high level that you are not waiting for him to open the door, you are knocking that door to the KINGDOM down.

Seeing is in the realm of revelation. Knocking and then entering brings you into the realm of visitation. But eventually you can visit enough and begin to know your way around the house building that eventually the owner says to you, "Why won't you stay here in a more permanent capacity?" Or maybe the owner feels you are here so much, you might as well get a key. You don't have to keep on knocking. You can just let yourself in with the keys of the KINGDOM. And you move from the realm of visitation to the realm of habitation. You must first ask to receive it. Then seek to find it. And lastly, you must knock to enter and eventually inherit and possess it. Being consistent with this protocol to inherit the KINGDOM will take you to the place where the King dwells so you can see and experience things from the KINGDOM perspective.

Phases of Seeking The KINGDOM

*One God and Father of all, who is **above all**, and **through all**, and **in you all**.*
(Ephesians 4:6)

Ephesians 4:6, I believe, gives a great picture of the KINGDOM of the Most High. It is his will to be above all, through all, and in us all so he can be all in all. As stated in the first chapter, the definition of the KINGDOM of the Most High that I was given by revelation of the Holy Spirit is the rule and reign of the Most High in you, over (above) you, and through you with the intention of being all in all. This is what I was taught by the Holy Spirit before

I even saw Ephesians 4:6 basically saying the same thing. This speaks to three arenas or phases of the KINGDOM that we should desire the presence of the rule and reign of the Most High to increase in our lives. There is a KINGDOM within you. There is a KINGDOM that is over and above you in the highest heavens. And there is a KINGDOM that the Most High desires to function and flow through you. This KINGDOM is through you because you are standing in as the middle person who is literally transferring that which is above to manifest in the earth. So you have the KINGDOM In You, the KINGDOM Above You, and the KINGDOM Through You. Concerning these three phases or facets of the KINGDOM, the next three chapters will provide more detail.

*8 Wherefore he saith, When he **ascended up on high**, he led captivity captive, and **gave gifts unto men**. 9 (Now that **he ascended**, what is it but that he also **descended first into the lower parts of the earth**? 10 He that descended is the same also that **ascended up far above all heavens**, that he might **fill all things**.) (Ephesians 4:8-10)*

I wanted to mention these three phases because we are talking here in this chapter about seeking first the KINGDOM. One might try to go straight to the KINGDOM through you. When in reality, there is an order. If we look at the scriptures in this section from Ephesians 4, we have an example of what Christ did and in what order. Christ is the firstborn of creation and he is the pattern Son. He is the way so we must follow his example. In these verses, we see that Christ ascended up on high and after he did that he was in a position to give gifts to men and to fill all things. But we also see before he ascended, he descended deep in the lower parts of the earth.

So the pattern is that he first descended in the lower parts. Then ascended to the high parts and then filled all things by releasing something from high to the earth. The lower parts represent within you. Sometimes we say the lower parts that Christ descended is like unto the "belly of the earth". Well the KINGDOM within includes our belly because Christ said out of our belly will flow rivers of living water. So we must descend or go deeper within and let the KINGDOM be established there first. Then once we come to a place of overcoming the flesh, having our hearts circumcised, and our minds renewed, we can then ascend to the aspect of the KINGDOM above. And once we operate in the high part of the KINGDOM, we can become conduits to bring heaven on earth as the KINGDOM fully operates through us. So we must migrate from the KINGDOM Within, to the KINGDOM Above, and then to the KINGDOM Through Us as we endeavor to seek the KINGDOM first.

Chapter 8 : The KINGDOM Within You

Neither shall they say, Lo here! or, lo there! for, behold, the **KINGDOM of God is within you**. *(Luke 17:21)*

At the end of the previous chapter, three phases or aspects of the KINGDOM of the Most High were discussed: 1) The KINGDOM Within You, 2) The KINGDOM Above You, and 3) The KINGDOM Through You. We can see in Luke 17:21, that the KINGDOM will not be found in a physical place but the place where we start to engage the KINGDOM of God is within us. There is an inner KINGDOM that the Heavenly Father desires to establish in your inner man that is the foundation needed to open up the door to the other aspects of the KINGDOM. The intent of this chapter is to share the different territories or components of the inner KINGDOM and how to allow the rule and reign of the Most High in you.

Deeper

Deep calleth unto deep *at the noise of thy waterspouts: all thy waves and thy billows are gone over me. (Psalms 42:7)*

The KINGDOM of the Most within you is something that he wants to be rooted deep within you. That is why Christ, the hope of glory, is within you. The scripture says that he stands at the door and knocks. He is within you waiting for you to turn inward to the Christ in you. And the more you turn to him, the more the door is opened and the veil is removed to give you access to him. The salvation of the Lord is not a surface thing. No, it is a deep thing. Not deep in the sense of being super spiritual or mystical in revelation. But it is deep because he is planted very deep within you so you can be rooted and grounded in him.

This makes me think about a spaghetti sauce company whose slogan was, "It's in there". Well, when you become alive with the Word of the KINGDOM and the Holy Spirit, Christ is in there but you have to be led by the Holy Spirit to seek for him and find him. If we were planting seeds and just threw them on the top of the soil, the harvest will not be plentiful. But when you dig deep and plant the seed, it gives that harvest a better chance. So we need the seed of Christ deep in us to conform us to the image of Christ.

We have to go deeper before we can go higher. When we deal with the KINGDOM within, we are going deeper. The trajectory of KINGDOM fullness is to go deeper, then Higher, and then lower and forward. It is like an athlete who is running before they try to jump high. Before they jump high, they must first somewhat squat down to maximize the jump. And when they ascend up in motion, they will eventually come down but hopefully in a spot ahead of where they originally jumped. You must overcome the KINGDOM within you before you are able to ascend higher in the KINGDOM above on a consistent basis. Deep calls to deep. Just as God is a spirit and they who worship him must worship him in the plane of spirit and truth. We must look deep within us to call out to Christ who is deep in us. And not only will we be able to call out to him but because we are in that position, we can hear and see him as well. Let's go deeper.

Image & Likeness First

*And God said, Let us make man **in our image, after our likeness**: and let them have dominion over the fish of the sea, and over the fowl of the air, and over the cattle, and over all the earth, and over every creeping thing that creepeth upon the earth. (Genesis 1:26)*

In the first chapter of Genesis in verse 26 where the intention of the KINGDOM was mentioned first, there is a cause and effect that is revealed. I mentioned this previously in Chapter 2. Before you can rule and have dominion you must first have the image and likeness of the Most High. Image speaks to what is seen either naturally or spiritually. Whereas, likeness speaks to your inner nature. If you don't have the image and nature of the Most High, then you cannot rule, reign, have dominion , or operate in authority.

For whom he did foreknow, he also **did predestinate** to be **conformed to the image of his Son**, that he might be the firstborn among many brethren. (Romans 8:29)

There is one image. In the beginning, he said, "make man in our image". It did not say "our images (plural)". It did not mean that Adam was to be made a man resulting from a mixture of different images. No!!! John 1:1 relates that in the beginning was the Word, and the Word was with God, and the Word was God. The image is the mark of what qualifies you in the royal family of God. That makes you a God kind or type. And before you think I am going on a strange tangent, in John 10:34, Christ states that in the law of

Moses, mankind are referred to as gods (lowercase g).

What do you think being made after his image and likeness means? He is our Father and we are his children. What children are not of the same species as their father? Dogs come from dogs. Cats come from cats. What do you think the Heavenly Father sees when he sees his children born again of his Spirit into his likeness and image? He sees himself in you. The image is what we see. That is why the Father and Son are one because he is the express image of the Father. When you see the Son, you have seen the Father. And his aim is for us to be one with him, that when people see us, they see them.

We were born again to bear the image of the Son which is the image from the beginning. I know if you ask someone what their call is, someone might say, "I am a pastor". Another might think their call is to be a prophet or an apostle. Another group might say I am called to the ministry of helps. That is fine and dandy but in the eyes of the Father there is truly one call and it is your first call. That call per Romans 8:29 is to be conformed to the image of the Son. The highest call is to reach the level of a mature son in the KINGDOM of the Most High.

So we have to be like him in every way. Not just from the perspective of the outward. But also we have to look and be like him in the inward parts. In the spiritual realm, everything is naked for observation. The Father, Christ, the Holy Spirit, angels, demons can truly see you because you are what you are within. Many on the outward can look holy and righteousness but it is what is within , that image and likeness, what really matters. There is no faking anyone who lives and walks in the spiritual realm. The Most High wants you to bear his image and likeness within and function in your holy call as a Son in his KINGDOM.

The First & Greatest Commandment of the KINGDOM

*And he answering said, Thou shalt **love the Lord thy God with all thy heart**, and with **all thy soul**, and with **all thy strength**, and with **all thy mind**; and thy neighbour as thyself. (Luke 10:27)*

The KINGDOM within is what we pursue first as we seek first the KINGDOM. The key word that jumps out and screams at me is "first". It is interesting that someone asked Christ what is the first and greatest commandment and his response was not a quote from Exodus 20 or Deuteronomy 5 where the Ten Commandments are housed. He did not go straight into "thou shall have no other gods before him". I believe what his answer was had similar meaning but Christ who was ushering in the KINGDOM of the Most High said it from a different perspective.

His answer from Deuteronomy 6 was that the first and greatest commandment is to love the Lord thy God with all your heart, all your soul, all your strength, and all your mind. The first commandment stated this way to me was all about the KINGDOM of God and territory. And the territories represented were not pieces of land in the physical. It was the territories of the KINGDOM within. The Lord your God wants to possess and have full ownership of your heart, mind, soul, and strength by a willful act of love from you. He does not want just part of it but he wants it all. We know the intention of the KINGDOM is for the Father to be all in all and the first commandment of the KINGDOM is about loving him with all and giving him all.

See, the Most High wants you to come to a place where you yield within you all your heart, mind, soul with all your strength, adoration, and love. In this, you are brought to a place where Christ reigns on a throne in your inner man and you become love. This love will then come from within and then overflow to the point where you will love your neighbor as yourself. Loving the Most High with your all and genuinely loving mankind with the love of the Most High is a sure indicator that the KINGDOM within has been activated and in full effect.

I believe the scripture of Luke 10:27 shows us at a high level the territories of the KINGDOM within which the Most High wants to rule, reign, and conquer. They are as follows:

- Your Heart
- Your Mind
- Your Soul
- Your Strength & Might

These aforementioned areas within you function also with another component that I will discuss later, is what I believe comprises the KINGDOM within. As we proceed in this chapter we will discuss these territories of the KINGDOM within at a high level.

The KINGDOM Within & Its Laws

This is the covenant that I will make with them after those days, saith the Lord, **I will put my laws into their hearts**, *and* **in their minds** *will* **I write them**;
(Hebrews 10:16)

Every phase or dimension of the KINGDOM has a facet of government which in turn correlates to laws and ordinances. The KINGDOM within is no different in this regard. The old covenant based on the law of Moses and the Levitical priesthood lacked in that it was an outward law that did not reign within. In most cases it was attempted to be fulfilled by the will and flesh of mankind. But Christ in the implementation of the KINGDOM had to make sure it was an inward work and make sure that it also brought in a new covenant and a new priesthood (Melchizedek). With this adjustment,t mankind can now have access to operate in a priesthood that functioned in heaven and on earth.

The new covenant as shown in Hebrews 10:16 was a covenant where the laws and KINGDOM government were written inwardly instead of being fixed on some stone tablets. On Mount Sinai many centuries ago, when the Most High gave the law to Moses, he wrote with his own finger on those tablets that could be broken and be destroyed. But now in the new KINGDOM covenant, Christ abiding within us as tabernacles is writing with his own finger on the tablets of our hearts and minds. This is such an exciting and beautiful picture to me. Because he had to go deeper within us to make sure we had a new nature and that he can reign from within. Because the KINGDOM of the Most High within must flow from inward to outward.

Outwardness does not matter in the way that we are saved by works. But we are saved by grace through faith UNTO good works. We are his workmanship because by the work of the Holy Spirit and the work of Christ inwardly, we are a new creation that gives glory to his name. A person will know that you have KINGDOM faith by your works of love that show on the outside. Instead of counting on people to go buy a bible and then to open it up to read it, then the laws written in us can show outside of us in our lives. This makes us to be the living letters and epistles that can be read by all men and women. And what lives inside us along with how we live will align with the words we preach. This is the KINGDOM flow to change us from inside out where we live and speak in a KINGDOM way.

I want to go back to the point that now in the KINGDOM, we are the temple and tabernacle of the Holy Spirit. Each tabernacle has three parts: the outer court, the Holy Place, and the Most Holy Place also known as the Holy of Holies. The outer court correlates with the flesh and body arena. The Holy Place deals with the arena of the soul and the mind where the Most Holy Place (Holy of Holies) speaks to the arena of the spirit and the heart.

Back to the main scripture of this section, it is the Most High intention to write his covenant laws in your mind and your heart. We see this symbolism in the picture of the tabernacle. In the mind and soul arena of the Holy Place, you have the table of shewbread present where the shewbread is renewed weekly. This represents the Word of the Most High being written in your mind and the engrafted Word in your soul. But being written in your soul and mind is not enough. It has to be written in your heart. And we see in the Most Holy Place, the ark of the covenant is present. And one of the items in the ark is the actual two tablets that were written on by the finger of God on Mount Sinai. This speaks to that inwardly in the realm of your heart with you being a tabernacle as well, that the Most High wants to write his laws in your heart. In order to have the KINGDOM reign within you, he must have his laws written in your hearts and minds.

KINGDOM of the Heart

Keep thy heart *with all diligence; for **out of it are the issues of life**. (Proverbs 4:23)*

Now that we have gone over that the Most High's goal of establishing his KINGDOM within is by writing his laws in the hearts and minds of people, let's look at the territories of the KINGDOM within. The word of the KINGDOM is a seed and to grow and expand anything, it must start with the seed or Word of the KINGDOM, his laws. And that seed has to start somewhere. The seed has to start in the garden of your heart. Your heart is a garden and whatever seeds are planted there will create a harvest that will show up in your outward life. As Proverbs 4:23 suggests, it is so important to keep your heart with all diligence because it is from the source of the heart that all things pertaining to life flows (issues) from.

The word "issues" here does not mean problems, drama, obstacles, or chaos.

But in Hebrew it means a source of outgoing flow. This is what the heart is. It is a source that whatever is in it, flows out to other areas and territories. And the Most High knows if he can sit on the throne of your heart, then he can possess and reign in the rest of you. If I had to give more context of what the heart is, then I would say just like in our physical body, the heart is the organ that pumps blood to all the extremities of the rest of the body. If you have a bad heart, your health will fail you. If there is an issue with your blood and the circulation, other areas of the body will suffer. Doctors can take a blood sample and run all types of tests and see your iron levels, determine paternity, and see if you are healthy or full of disease. The heart is so important not just in your physical body but also when it comes to the KINGDOM within.

Everything flows from the heart. I believe the heart is a component of your spirit man that is a liaison to your soul where everything starts in the heart and flows to the soul which then downstream impacts what physical actions you employ in your body. The heart, maybe shockingly to some, is the thinking aspect of your spirit. This is why the scriptures declare that as a man thinks in his heart, so is he. Whatever is going on in your heart, is the truth of who you are. That is when the Most High judges, he judges the heart and not just actions.

The heart is the thinking center of your spirit, where the mind is the thinking component of your soul, and your physical brain is the control center of your body. The heart is the seat of your motives and intentions. Staying with the agriculture analogy, the heart is the garden where the seeds of the Most High or the enemy are planted and motives and intentions are watered to come alive and produce fruit. When we talk about the fruit of the Spirit like love, peace, longsuffering, goodness, meekness, and the sort, it is produced in the garden of the heart. When other fleshly seeds are planted, then eventually downstream, the work of the flesh will manifest in your life.

Everything about your life, good or bad, flows from your heart which makes it so important to guard and keep your heart. In Proverbs 4:23, the word "keep" means to guard, watch over, and protect. This is very similar to the command the Most High gave Adam in the beginning that he is to keep and guard the garden of Eden. Your heart is a garden that must be protected at all cost and it is your job to make sure the right things are being planted and rooted in the garden. And once the right things are planted, then you will have to everyday allow time to let Christ and the Holy Spirit, prune, fertilize, and water the heart with the washing of the water of the Word so that a tree of life can exist and grow in your heart.

*And let the peace of God **rule in your hearts**, to the which also ye are called in one body; and be ye thankful. (Colossians 3:15)*

There is a KINGDOM and throne in your heart. The peace of the Most High is supposed to rule in your hearts. Where there is rule, there is a throne. And where there is a throne, there is a KINGDOM. The aim is for Christ to sit on the throne of your heart and not the enemy or even your fleshly self. The rule doesn't stop with Christ sitting on the throne of your heart. But just like in the KINGDOM sense, the Father let Christ sit on the right side of him and also how Christ is inviting us to have a place with him on his throne, the same applies to the heart. It starts off with Christ reigning in your heart, but as you mature, you also co-reign with him on that throne.

*A **good man out of the good treasure of his heart** bringeth forth **that which is good;** and an e**vil man out of the evil treasure of his heart** bringeth forth **that which is evil:** for of the abundance of the heart his mouth speaketh. (Luke 6:45)*

The heart is also like a treasure chest where either the treasure can be evil or it can be good. And whatever is in this treasure chest, determines what will come out of it to be seen by others. Everything that proceeds out of mankind starts from the heart. Once again the heart is the source. With the fall of Adam, it allowed the heart of man to become evil but now with the KINGDOM coming alive within you, the good Shepherd can now plant good treasures within you.

The heart in this KINGDOM transition must go through a process in a number of ways. From a garden perspective, everything that is evil must be uprooted and new things must be planted. This takes time. But also that which is dirty , must be cleansed with fresh water. The water can be the Word of God or that from the Holy Spirit because rivers of living water are supposed to flow out of your belly to cleanse your heart. God also desires your heart to be pure where there is no mixture of his KINGDOM and another KINGDOM. This takes time and a pure heart is key when it comes to the KINGDOM as we will discuss later in this book. And lastly, your heart needs to be circumcised. Just as the foreskin of the penis is removed at the head of the penis, the same must happen with the heart. Circumcision of the heart by the sword of the Spirit, also known as the Word is sharp enough to remove the fleshly aspects of your heart so that the true head and King of Christ can be revealed in you. The planting and the establishing of the KINGDOM in the heart is paramount if the other territories of the KINGDOM within must be conquered.

KINGDOM of the Mind

In a presidential election, especially in the United States, the candidates in their strategy understand that there are key states that they must give attention to, to win the whole election. In a war, great strategists of combat understand that certain battlegrounds or forts are key to victory and gaining ground. It is the same with the KINGDOM of the Most High. With the KINGDOM within, possessing the stronghold of the heart and the mind is pivotal to everything. That is why the new covenant is to write the laws (government) in the heart and mind. The heart is the headquarters of the spirit and the mind is the headquarters of the soul and he needs a branch of government in the heart and the mind. It is like the executive and the legislative branch working together to establish laws for a government. Rule in the heart will not be optimum and impactful if rule of his KINGDOM does not occur in the mind as well.

*4 (For the weapons of our warfare are not carnal, but mighty through God to **the pulling down of strong holds;**) 5 **Casting down** **imaginations**, and **every high thing that exalteth itself against the knowledge of God**, and **bringing into captivity every thought to the obedience of Christ**; (2 Corinthians 10:4-5)*

The enemy even understands the priority of having representation in the heart and mind. The enemy comes immediately to steal the word of the KINGDOM so it does not take root in your heart. Sometimes we look at the term strongholds as a bad term, but in all truth, it just means having a positioning of strength and influence in a certain area. So the Most High wants to have a stronghold in you. These are yokes. The yoke and stronghold of the enemy causes bondage, but the yoke of Christ brings peace and liberty. For there to be reign in the KINGDOM within, there must be control of the strongholds in the heart and the mind. Whoever has control of those two will eventually get the rest of the territories.

I love the first scripture of this section in 2 Corinthians 10 because it shows the war strategy of the Most High when it comes to the KINGDOM territory of the mind. In the heart, the strategy is to uproot, replant, and prune. In the mind, the strategy is basically the same where he wants to pull down all the strongholds of the enemy and then rebuild his own strongholds hence the need of writing his laws in your mind. What I love about it is that in the KINGDOM, there is violence and this text paints a picture of a mighty King coming in and with strength and power violently pulling down the strongholds of the enemy.

Our King is one who wants all so he doesn't stop there. He continues and then also casts down all imaginations and all thoughts that exalts itself against the knowledge of Christ as King to the end of bringing every imagination and thought under complete obedience to Christ the King. Remember the KINGDOM has the intent to be all in all. The King will not rest until he takes all that is against his KINGDOM into captivity and bring it into subjection to him. This is part of the KINGDOM that he is establishing within you.

*1 I beseech you therefore, brethren, by the mercies of God, that ye **present your bodies a living sacrifice**, holy, **acceptable unto God,** which is your reasonable service. 2 And **be not conformed to this world**: but be ye **transformed by the renewing of your mind**, that ye may prove what is **that good, and acceptable, and perfect, will of God.** Romans 12:1-2)*

In a KINGDOM, it is about what the King desires and what is acceptable to him. In Romans 12, we see that our King is desiring for us to present ourselves as a living sacrifice. That means you need to present your heart and mind as a sacrifice. Why? So it can be acceptable to the King. And also, you can align with the acceptable, good, and perfect will and desire of that King. But to do this, you have to have a renewed mind. You can't function in the old mind that was in agreement with the enemy's world system. You can no longer be formed by the world system of the enemy and allow Christ in you to renew your mind. The Most High wants you to stop flowing in a carnal mind that lives for the world system of the enemy and to flow in a spiritual mind that brings new life to you. For a carnal mind produces death, but the mind that is aligned to the Spirit of God produces life. The King wants you to have the mind of Christ and the path to do this is through meditation of the Word. It is through the meditation of the Word, that you eat of the table of shewbread, and his Word and laws are written in your mind to cause change within you and through you.

*5 **Let this mind be in you, which was also in Christ Jesus:** 6 Who, **being in the form of God**, thought it not robbery to be equal with God: 7 But made himself of no reputation, and took upon him the form of a servant, and was made in the likeness of men: 8 And being found in fashion as a man, he **humbled himself,*** *and became obedient unto death, even the death of the cross.* ***9 Wherefore God also hath highly exalted him***, *and given him **a name which is above every name**: **10** That at the name of Jesus **every knee should bow,** of things in heaven, and things in earth, and things under the earth; (Phiippians 2:5-10)*

The KINGDOM takeover of the Most High within you is not automatic. You have to let this mind be in you which is also in Christ Jesus (Yeshua). You have to yield and bow to the King and his KINGDOM. Even though you are a joint heir and also a KINGDOM Son to the Heavenly Father, you must humble yourself like Christ did to the cross. You want to reign in the KINGDOM of our Father, we have to learn to humble ourselves. We have to have the mind of humility.

The reward to Christ and his humility was that he was highly exalted and given a name above every other name that at the mention of that name every knee bowed to his kingship and dominion. As we follow the patterns of Christ, we will become just like him and we will abide in him and the same authority that he operates in will be given to us to operate as kings and priests. In that same manner, every enemy will recognize the power of his name and bow to that name in us, as we humble ourselves to the King. We will be highly exalted as well to rule and reign with Christ in his KINGDOM. We can use that same family name that is above every other name, and the enemy and every evil agent of the KINGDOM in darkness will bow to us. We need to have the mind of Christ and let him rule in the territory of the mind.

KINGDOM of the Soul

The King of Kings wants it all. He wants the heart and the mind and the entirety of your soul. I believe that we are a tripartite being of spirit, soul, and body and in the KINGDOM of the Most High, he wants your spirit man joined to the Holy Spirit to reign as King and Master. And then have it where your soul is the servant and your body is the slave in a sense. The spirit part if born again is full of light and life and is made in the substance and likeness of the Most High. But the soul is the part that makes you somewhat unique from others from a spiritual perspective.

The soul is the seat of your will, intellect, and emotions. It is in the soul where you filter what came from your spirit and heart and make decisions on how to proceed. In your soul, is your will where you choose to be a servant to the King or to do things your own way. Also, in your soul is where you decide what expression you will walk in when it comes to the state of your soul emotionally. Out of your soul flows your emotions if you are in peace, happy, sad, angry, loving, and so forth. Also, in your soul, as it gets the information from the spiritual side of things, your intellect is at work to rationalize and interpret it with logic to make sense. The soul is important because this is where you have the power of choice to choose what will be sent to your body to do and perform.

The King wants you to love him with ALL your soul. He wants you to love him in your will. He wants you to love him with your intellect and reasoning. He wants you to love him with all your emotions. And by loving him with all of this , this is how he reigns though the soul. From the spirit perspect, the spirit is the offspring of the King but the soul is the servant to the King.

Have you ever heard of the bondservant? The bondservant was a servant who once was forced to do whatever his master told him to do but eventually the Master decided to give him freedom. But the bondservant did not take this new found freedom to do whatever he wanted but he chose to say I love my master and will choose to still be under his control. This is what the King is looking for in our souls for us to be bondservants who choose to love the King in our obedience and servitude.

*Wherefore **lay apart all filthiness and superfluity of naughtiness**, and **receive with meekness the engrafted word**, which is able to **save your souls**.*
(James 1:21)

So in James 1:21, it is not saying that the King will automatically take over. No, it is implying that if you want the King of glory to reign in your soul you have to choose to lay aside all flow of filthiness and naughtiness. A decision has to be made within you. Choose you this day whom you will serve. You have the motives and intentions in your heart but in your soul you have to choose who you are going to serve. I know many who have the right motives and intentions but were not able to choose to carry out what they were supposed to. It is in the soul that by laying aside filthiness and receiving with meekness the engrafted (inward) Word of God that salvation will spring forth in your soul. And the King of Kings will take kingship over the territory of the soul.

The KINGDOM by Strength (Force)

Another territory that the Most High wants to reign in is your strength and might. One version says to love the Lord thy God with all your strength and another place says might but it is the same Greek word. It is the Greek word "ischys" which means ability, force, power, strength, and might.

I want to key in on the meaning that says strength means "power". We know that the KINGDOM of God suffers violence and the violent take it by force. I know we say "not by power, not by might but by the Spirit". It is true it has to be by the Spirit of the Most High. But he still wants to partner with your might, strength, and might. Your strength and might still has to step up to the plate. He still wants to co-partner with you in this KINGDOM journey and he wants all your strength and might even when you feel weak. The key is to be strong in the power of his might and strength and not out of your own.

I believe that strength and might goes along with what passion you are bringing to the table when it comes to your love for the King and his KINGDOM. Strength is powered by passion and desire. How much do you want it? How much do you love him? How hungry and thirsty are you for this thing called the KINGDOM? Are you desperate for the things of the KINGDOM? Do you understand that he wants it all? Do you understand that without him, there is nothing? These are the questions that strength and might within you might ask when it comes to the KINGDOM.

I often use the example of you going to a sports game and seeing the super fan who is cheering with all their strength and might even to the point of hoarseness or embarrassment. But they don't care because they are in such support of their favorite team, they are going to give all that it takes. Some will go shirtless and put on face paint or wear some ridiculous wig or costume. Some will stand in line overnight in the cold and rain to get the best tickets and seats to show they are down for their favorite player or team.

When it comes to the territory of strength and might within you , our King wants to know if you are down with the King and if you are willing to let anybody and everybody know it. Are you down for the King even if no one else sees you? Are you full of passion, might and giving your all if it's just you? For the King it takes sacrifice and with that sacrifice the King is looking for you to put him first, give him your all, and to give him your best.

I think one more angle I want to put emphasis on, was that strength meant ability. The word "ability" puts in mind your strengths, gifts and talents that the Most High has allowed to function in your life. The gifts and callings of the Most High are without repentance so they will flow in your life from birth with or without your commitment to the King. But when it says to love him with all your strength and your might, I see an implication that he wants you to love him with your gifts, talents, and all your ability. The King gifted you according to the counsel of his will and has a purpose for those abilities. Are you letting the King rule and reign even in your talents and gifts? The King wants to reign in your strength and might within you. And it is by strength, might, and power that you will work with the Holy Spirit to allow the KINGDOM of the Most High to invade your inner life even more.

KINGDOM of the Tongue

In Mark 16, Christ told us to them that believe they will cast out devils and lay hands on the sick and they will recover amongst other things. But by revelation of the Holy Spirit, it was highlighted to me that it says they will speak with new tongues. I know this is used to emphasize the baptism of the Holy Spirit. But also as there are probably at least seven degrees of revelation to every scripture in the bible, the Holy Spirit wants us to know that he wants our tongues to be made new. It is the purpose of the King and his KINGDOM to eventually some type of way to impact our tongue and the words we speak.

*2 For in many things we offend all. If any man **offend not in word**, the same is a **perfect man, and able also to bridle the whole body**. 3 Behold, we put bits in the horses' mouths, that they may obey us; and we turn about their whole body. 4 Behold also the ships, which though they be so great, and are driven of fierce winds, **yet are they turned about with a very small helm**, whithersoever the governor listeth. 5 Even so t**he tongue is a little member, and boasteth great things**. Behold, how great a matter a little fire kindleth! 6 And **the tongue is a fire, a world of iniquity**: so is the tongue among our members, that it **defileth the whole body**, and **setteth on fire the course of nature**; and it is set on fire of hell. (James 3:2-6)*

The tongue is not listed in the areas in Luke 10:27 to love the Lord with but I want to add it as a component of the KINGDOM within. In James 3, the scripture listed before this paragraph, the tongue's importance is shown. If a man does not offend the KINGDOM in word, then this same man has reached a level of maturity in the eyes of the King. It continues to hint that if the tongue is under control, then it will also bridle the whole body. Under control of who? The King. The tongue is compared to a small helm that guides a big ship. The tongue is a little member but it has great power. If the tongue is filled with iniquity, then it is a fire and can defile the whole body. It is not what you eat that defiles the body but what you speak with your tongue that can defile you.

__Death and life__ are in the __power of the tongue__: and they that love it shall eat __the fruit__ thereof. (Proverbs 18:21)

The tongue can be dangerous and has the power to bring death or life into your life or any situation. So now you should understand why Christ said to those who believe the gospel of the KINGDOM, that he is coming for their tongues and words to become new. See Christ understood that the tongue if renewed and used properly can be utilized to manifest the KINGDOM of God from within and communicate the will of God that is higher to manifest in the earth.

It is through our tongues and mouth that we praise the Lord in word and song. It is through our tongue that we can make declarations and decrees to manifest the KINGDOM of the Most High in our lives and others. It is through our tongue that we can change the atmosphere. It is through the tongue that we can cast out devils and scatter the enemy. It is through the tongue that we can either bless or curse. It is through our words that it impacts what fruit bears all around us. They that love death , will speak words of death and experience the wages of death. But those who love life, will speak life, and eat the fruit of life. The King wants to reign in the territory of our mouth, tongue, and words.

Heart and Tongue Connection

*A good man out of the good treasure of his heart bringeth forth that which is good; and an evil man out of the evil treasure of his heart bringeth forth that which is evil: **for of the abundance of the heart his mouth speaketh.** (Luke 6:45)*

Note that the first territory of the KINGDOM within we discussed was the heart and the last one we will discuss in this chapter is the tongue or the mouth. I mentioned this because the flow of the KINGDOM is from the first to the last. He wants that which he started to be the same in the end. And therefore, there is a connection to what is in your heart and to what you end up speaking out of your mouth. Luke 6:45 was featured in a previous section of this chapter in terms that the judgment of a good or evil man depends on their heart. But the last part of that scripture elaborates that it is out of the abundance of your heart that the mouth speaks. If you spoke it, then it is on some level in abundance, not a little, in your heart. So that which is in your heart will eventually flow through the territories of the KINGDOM within and make it to your mouth and tongue.

*Let the **words of my mouth**, and the **meditation of my heart**, be **acceptable in thy sigh**t, O Lord, my strength, and my redeemer. (Psalms 19:14)*

There is a connection between the tongue and mouth. There is a principle of witness and agreement that works in the KINGDOM of the Most High that a thing should be established by two or three witnesses. Another aspect is that if any two or more things touch and agree according to the will of God , it shall come to pass. So the two things that need to be aligned to establish something is your heart and your tongue.

One of my favorite scriptures is above in Psalms 19:14. I pray this every day with my wife and the rest of my family. It is actually how I end most of my prayers. My hope is that the words of my mouth and the meditation of my heart will be acceptable to the Highest King. The Most High judges not by the outward but by the heart but also we are told that every idle word that comes out of our mouth will be judged by him as well. The thrust of the KINGDOM within is to have the heart and tongue align and touch and agree that mighty things can be birthed and accomplished in the KINGDOM of God on the earth.

*Now unto him that is able to do exceeding abundantly above all that **we ask or think**, according to **the power that worketh in us**, (Ephesians 3:20)*

Even with salvation, it is not only believing in your heart. But it is also the alignment of the confession with your mouth that brings you to a place of newness of the KINGDOM in your life. Ephesians 3:20 shows the powerful connection of the mouth (tongue) and the heart. The mouth does the asking and the heart and mind do the thinking. Remember as a man thinks in his heart, so is he. It is when the two align that the Most High can do exceedingly and abundantly and ABOVE all that we ask and think. We have to be careful what we are meditating on in our heart. We also have to be careful what we are asking and declaring out of our mouths because these two decide what power is working in us. Out the heart are the issues (flow) of life and life and death is in the power of the tongue. So the effectiveness of the power of the KINGDOM working within you depends on the heart and tongue alignment to the King.

All Territories of the KINGDOM Within Are Linked

I believe there is an inward to outward flow of the KINGDOM within that starts from the spiritual heart to the mind through the soul that eventually flows to what comes out of our mouth and impacts our actions. Apostle Paul said in one of his letters that we believe (in his heart) so therefore we speak (2 Corinthians 4:13). When all the territories of the KINGDOM within come into oneness, alignment, and agreement, the power and glory of the KINGDOM will be resident in your life.

Our intentions and motives of the heart impacts our imagination and thoughts of our mind. So we need the Word of the Most High to discern and be able to separate what is spiritual and soulish. Our thoughts impact our words. Our words impact our actions. And our words and actions frame the world we live in and our reality. We have what we say. But what we say and speak need to come from a higher source of the one whose ways and thoughts are higher than ours. We speak from within ourselves and also based on what we experience. So the key is to allow the KINGDOM of Christ to reign within and this will set the stage to introduce to you his KINGDOM above you.

Chapter 9 : The KINGDOM Above You

*1 If ye then be risen with Christ, **seek those things which are above**, where Christ sitteth on the right hand of God. 2 Set **your affection on things above**, not on things on the earth.*
(Colossians 3:1-2)

The spread of the KINGDOM of the Most High in your life starts within, but it eventually leads you to the KINGDOM above you. There is so much I can say about the KINGDOM above us but the purpose of this chapter is to keep things at a high level to make certain points to encourage you to seek the higher things of the KINGDOM of the Most High. It is the will of the Father to have his KINGDOM children to mature to manifested Sons in all of creation. He desires that we experience KINGDOM fullness in all aspects and phases of his KINGDOM even as we are living on the earth now.

In John 14, Christ lets us know that our Father which resides in heaven above, that his house has many mansions, rooms, and dimensions. And the point of the blood sacrifice of Christ was to remove the veil and grant us access to all layers of the KINGDOM, within, above, and through us.

In Colossians 3:1-2, Apostle Paul admonishes us as believers to seek those things above and to set our affections on things above. Why if, as some believe, we are supposed to wait until we die to experience heaven, are we being told to seek the things above? It would be a cruel thing for him to suggest that we seek something that we can't find at that moment especially since Christ said that if we seek, we shall find. We are told to seek first the KINGDOM and his righteousness (right standing and access). We are also told to seek those things above. Maybe seeking those things above and seeking first the KINGDOM and righteousness are one in the same.

I will even go a step further. Apostle Paul in those verses tell us what level above he is talking about. Some might say oh seeking the things above is to stay positive and keep your head up. Some might say it means to rise above the evils of this world and live in a plane that is higher. But the scripture says seek those things that are above WHERE Christ sits on the right hand of God the Father. So we are being told to seek the throne room of the Most High not in some strange figurative sense, but in reality in the KINGDOM's spiritual realm. Then it adds to it and says your affection and passion should be above and not in this world. I am here to tell you in this book that there is much more than you can imagine that the KINGDOM of the Most High has made available to you.

Invitation to Come Higher

*After this I looked, and, behold, **a door was opened in heaven**: and the first voice which I heard was as it were of a trumpet talking with me; which said, **Come up hither**, and **I will shew thee things** which must be hereafter. (Revelation 4:1)*

In this verse in the book of Revelation, John the Revelator experienced a door or portal opening in heaven and heard a voice extend him an invitation to come up hither (higher) so he can be shown some things. This is not the only time in the book of Revelation that he is granted this invitation to come higher. Our God is not a respecter of persons. This invitation was not only for John. This invitation is for you as a KINGDOM believer.

We have seen Enoch be lifted up in this realm above. We have seen Isaiah and Ezeiel lifted up and experience the throne room and temple of the Most High. Apostle Paul in 2 Corinthians 12 talked about how he knew a man in Christ who was caught up in third heavens. Many think he was talking about himself. So we even see a pattern for those who even before Christ died for us that they were able to have visitations in the realm above. And after Christ died and rose again, we see that some were able to ascend in the KINGDOM above and have more than visitation. There is a call to you and me to come higher and let's ascend the hill of the Lord.

We start deeper, but deeper will lead us to that which is higher. Oh Mighty God, lead us to the rock that is higher than us. He is the Most High God. His glory is above the heavens. He dwells in the Highest of the heavens. In the Lord's prayer, we start off with "Our Father which art in Heaven" to show us where our focus and affection should be. Remember, the goal was to reconcile us back to the Father and bring us back to Eden and beyond. He did not just say the KINGDOM of God within you is at hand. But all throughout the book of Matthew, we are told the "KINGDOM of Heaven" is at hand and available. It is time now through the blood of Christ to accept the invitation and seek those things which are above and come up higher.

Overcoming Sons

*He that **overcometh shall inherit all things;** and **I will be his God**, and **he shall be my son**. (Revelation 21:7)*

One thing we have now is the access to that which is above in the KINGDOM above. It is just not in the fact that it exists above or that he just wants us to tour the territories of the KINGDOM above. It is more than that. He is calling us to be joint heirs with him and to reign and rule there as well. He is our God (King) and our Father. He wants us to get the KINGDOM aspect but not neglect that we are his offspring who is calling us to be about the Father's business which is the KINGDOM of the Most High above.

The KINGDOM is to some invisible. To us the KINGDOM is above us. It does not seem easily accessible and guess what? We have an enemy who does not want us to see the invisible or ascend to that which is above and to continue to be caught in the web and illusion of his world system. But ever since Christ came on the scene, the Most High is calling for KINGDOM Sons to press into the KINGDOM and overcome the world, the enemy, and the flesh so you can fully enter in and possess (inherit) the KINGDOM of the Most High.

Inheritance and possession of all things KINGDOM only comes through overcoming. I know there might be some saying why are you not talking about the bride of Christ and all that stuff? Well when you take on the KINGDOM perspective and put in mind that the Hebrew culture was a picture of the KINGDOM above on some level, then inheritance and reigning speaks from a masculine side. In America and some other countries in these modern times, if a married man who had sons and daughters had great possessions died, then most likely a big portion of the inheritance will go right to the wife. But in biblical times and even in some African and Middle Eastern countries today, the inheritance would have gone to the firstborn son and he would make sure the rest of the family would get their portion.

I say that to emphasize that when I am talking about KINGDOM Sons, I am not talking about your biological gender in the physical. But I am talking about who you are and what your positioning is in the spirit. The KINGDOM is not about a physical bloodline, race, ethnicity, or gender but about if you have been born again to be conformed to the image of the Son. Because it is that image of the Son that reigns. A discussion about being a bride is good for topics of intimacy, holiness, purity and oneness but when we are talking about KINGDOM and reigning, we are talking about mature Sons in the Spirit. The whole of creation is not looking for the bride of Christ. It is looking for the manifestation of the Sons of God.

Do you have the royal bloodline in you? Are you conformed to the image of the Son, and not a daughter? (I want you to think spiritual and not physical.) I need you to grab this by the Spirit. As the firstborn Son overcame, you must become a mature son by overcoming. And this overcoming will cause you to arise and elevate to a place of authority because now you are like Christ. The call to be a Son is the number one call. He wants Sons so you can reign and rule in his KINGDOM.

Without going into too much detail, it has been revealed to me that mature Sons engage with the Father in Heaven and in his throne room. And there are four faceted aspects of the office of a Son. You have the Lion who represents the King aspect. You have the Ox who represents the priest aspect. Then you have the Eagle who represents the prophet or having the ability to see from high up from the perspective of the Father. In other words, this is knowing the mind, wisdom, and will of God. And lastly, you have the Man who represents being a son who is made in the image of the Son and is a sent one (apostle) to bring salvation of the KINGDOM to earth and all creation.

Some might say, isn't the apostle and prophet part of the fivefold ministry we see so many as part of today. My answer is no. The fourfold ministry of the Son exists in the realm of the Father and a son is sent forth from the loins of the Father. But the fivefold ministry is really the ascension gifts issued from Christ Jesus as gifts to men to help to conform people to the image and stature of Christ and for the perfecting of the saints and the church. They should be pointing to Christ, the things above and teach people how to ascend in the things of the KINGDOM. Grab this!!! The fivefold ministry of ascension gifts is for the church. The fourfold dimension of the office of a Son is for the KINGDOM and all creation! The fivefold is temporal in a sense because it has an "until" attached to it in Ephesians 4. But the office of a manifested Son is eternal. We are called to overcome and become Sons who walk in power and glory just like our elder brother.

Seven Spirits of God

1 And there shall come forth a rod out of the stem of Jesse, and a Branch shall grow out of his roots: 2 And the **spirit of the Lord** *shall rest upon him,* **the spirit of wisdom** *and* **understanding***, the* **spirit of counsel** *and might, the* **spirit of knowledge** *and of the* **fear of the Lord***; 3 And shall make him of quick understanding in the fear of the Lord: and* **he shall not judge after the sight of his eyes***, neither* **reprove after the hearing of his ears***: 4 But with righteousness shall he* **judge** *the poor, and* **reprove** *with equity for the meek of the earth: and he shall smite the earth: with the rod of his mouth, and with the breath of his lips shall he slay the wicked.*
(Isaiah 11:1-4)

I am so thankful for the Holy Spirit who is our key helper and comforter as we journey through the KINGDOM journey within. But as the proverb says, "it takes a village" and as we begin to enter and become more aware of the KINGDOM above, we begin to engage the seven spirits of Yahweh. They exist in the realm of the Father to teach and point you to the Father and give you guidance in your maturation process of becoming a Son. The

Holy Spirit points you to the realm of Christ as his job is to not speak of himself but of Christ. But the seven spirits of Yahweh the Father points you to the realm of the Father and your sonship. Just as Christ Jesus (Yeshua) had rested on him the seven spirits of Yahweh to be the Son of God that he was called to, it is evident that we must engage them in our rise to sonship as well. In sonship we need to know how to judge, reprove, and legislate when it comes to the KINGDOM.

*1 Now I say, That **the heir**, as long as he is a **child, differeth nothing from a servant**, though **he be lord of all;** 2 But is **under tutors and governors** until the **time appointed of the father**. (Galatians 4:1-2)*

In the beginning stages of being born again, we are still as little children in the KINGDOM even though we are heirs. But as long as we are in a certain state, we do not differ anything from a servant in the KINGDOM because the truth is that you must go through servanthood before you walk fully in sonship. But in our maturation, the Father has also given us tutors and governors such as the seven spirits of Yahweh to train and mentor us in all things concerning sonship. To go to another level, we need the seven spirits of Yahweh to go from gifts of the Spirit to the fruit of the Spirit to KINGDOM sonship by the seven spirits of Yahweh. Below is the list of these seven spirits of Yahweh and at high level their role in preparing and maturing us in sonship:

- The Spirit of the Lord: The spirit of the Lord mandates us for sonship as it teaches us about positional dominion and how to see the reality of the dimension of the KINGDOM. It also focuses on how to exercise dominion on the face of the earth.
- The Spirit of Wisdom: The spirit of wisdom equips us for positions as it teaches us how to judge and bring justice and how to bring divine order in the KINGDOM realm. It also focuses on what to do in the realm of rulership as a son.

- The Spirit of Understanding: The spirit of understanding authorizes us for sonship. It teaches us how to use what we have at the right time.
- The Spirit of Counsel: The spirit of counsel prepares us for sonship as it teaches us which way to rule as a son and how to access the counsel and consultation of the Father
- The Spirit of Might: The spirit of might reveals us for position as it teaches us how to exercise the supernatural realm of the Most High to reveal his power and might. It also has expertise on the secrets on how to war in the spirit realm.
- The Spirit of Knowledge: The spirit of knowledge empowers us for sonship as it shows us how to gain access to the knowledge of our Father and how to apply it in the world around us.
- The Spirit of the Fear of the Lord: The spirit of the fear of the Lord brings accountability for sonship as we are shown the understanding of the awe and wonder of the Most High. It is all about the person of the Most High teaches us the realms of holiness, intimacy, worship, reverence, and righteousness.

As you can see there is some overlap between the seven spirits of Yahweh and that is because sometimes they are most likely to work in pairs as implied by the groupings in Isaiah 11. There is more that can be said but I wanted to point out that we need to engage the KINGDOM above so we can walk in the fullness of what we are called to.

The Melchizedek Priesthood

*9 And **being made perfect**, he became the **author of eternal salvation unto all them that obey him**; 10 Called of God an **high priest after the order of Melchisedec**. (Hebrews 5:9-10)*

Why did Christ have to be made perfect and why did he learn obedience and perfection by the things he suffered? Because the sacrifice had to be perfect. But also there was a change of the priesthood. In the Levitical priesthood the high priest had to present to God for his sins and others many times, but in the Melchizedek priesthood the high priest presented himself for the sins of others and not himself only one time. Under the old covenant, there was the temporal Levitical priesthood, but now there is the eternal Melchizedek priesthood that is linked to the KINGDOM of the Most High. In the Old covenant you had one bloodline for the priests and another for the kingship, but with the Melchizedek priesthood the kingship and the priesthood combine under one bloodline, the bloodline of Christ.

What does this have to do with the KINGDOM above? Well we are called to be a royal priesthood which is part king and part priest in function. As you saw from the Sonship section, two of the fourfold facets of sonship are kingship and priesthood. The Father orchestrated that his Sons of the KINGDOM will be also priests and kings of the Melchizedek priesthood. Christ is the pattern and the high priest but every high priest has priests that work with them. He is the King of us who are kings. He is the Lord of us who are lords. But also he is the High Priest of us who are priests. This is part of the responsibility of being a mature and manifested son of the Most High.

*If therefore perfection were by the Levitical priesthood, (for under it the people received the law,) what further need was there that **another priest should rise after the order of Melchisedec**, and not be called after the order of Aaron?*
(Hebrews 7:11)

This priesthood operates in the realm above where the levitical priesthood only was restricted to the earth realm. There is work to do for the KINGDOM Sons in the KINGDOM above. The Levitical realm works in the earthly temple and tabernacle but the kings and priests of the Melchizedek order function in the Heavenly Temple in the Heavenly Jerusalem. This priesthood order of Christ works high above to bring judgment and rule to the earth below. Levitcial was the Most High meeting mankind where they were but Melchizedek is Sons arising to meet the Father where he is.

*And **hath made us kings and priests** unto **God and his Father**; to him be glory and **dominion** for ever and ever. Amen. (Revelation 1:6)*

There might be the following inquiries. Isn't the Melchizedek order just for Christ? Show us where in the bible where we are a part of this order. And if it is for us, then isn't this down the line in time in the future? Well Revelation 1:6 reveals that Christ has made us kings and priests. And notice the tense here. It is past tense. He has made us through Calvary kings and priests. So, no it is not just for Christ Jesus. It is for us to function in it now. Christ is aligned with the Melchizedek order but we have to remember Christ is a multi membered body where Christ Jesus is the head and we are the body. The head is the high priest of this order and we the body are the priests. The head is the King of kings and the body is the kings under the head King. We need to know the KINGDOM above to fully walk in our offices as kings and priests in this present time.

KINGDOM Ascension Above

*22 But ye are come unto **mount Sion**, and unto the city of the living God, **the heavenly Jerusalem**, and to an **innumerable company of angels**, 23 To the **general assembly and church of the firstborn**, which are written in heaven, and to **God the Judge of all**, and to the **spirits of just men made perfect**, 24 And to **Jesus the mediator of the new covenant**, and to the **blood of sprinkling**, that speaketh better things than that of Abel. (Hebrews 12:22-24)*

In the previous text of Hebrews 12, the author here is contrasting the old covenant way where they had to encounter a dreadful sight in the earth to encounter the Father and how he spoke things that they could not take to heart so much so that they told Moses you go to talk to him and tell us what he said. But in the new KINGDOM way, the author is saying now you are able to come to the KINGDOM above. You have access and it will not be scary but the KINGDOM is righteousness, peace, and joy.

A lot of times we talk about the death, burial, and the resurrection of Christ and then from there some might say we need to identify with Christ Jesus (Yeshua) in all those phases. But we have forgotten a phase and that phase is ascension. After the resurrection, he ascended to the Father to take his place on his throne. Christ is the pattern and the first born who is the way, the truth, and the life. We need to also know that we have been called to ascend to the KINGDOM above and be one with the Father and Son. As presented in the later part of Hebrews 12, there are territories and areas in the KINGDOM above that we are called to engage and interact with. They are the following:

- Mount Sion/Zion
- The Heavenly Jerusalem
- The Heavenly Father Who Is Also Judge Of All
- A Company Of Angels
- The Gathering And Church Of The Firstborn
- Spirits Of Just Men Made Perfect
- Jesus Christ (Yeshua), The Mediator Of The New Covenant
- The Sprinkling Of The Blood Of Christ That Speaks Better Things Of Abel

This is not an exhaustive list as there are definitely other aspects of the KINGDOM above that we can engage as KINGDOM Sons but I want to use this scriptural context to give a high level overview. Some of these areas I have had interaction with and still learning and pressing in to walk in the fullness of the KINGDOM.

Mt Zion

And **many nations shall come**, and say, Come, and **let us go up to the mountain of the Lord**, and to the house of the God of Jacob; and **he will teach us of his ways**, and **we will walk in his paths: for the law shall go forth of Zion**, and the word of the Lord from Jerusalem. (Micah 4:2)

Zion is the mountain of the Most High. Yes on the earth, there was a hill in Jerusalem of ancient Israel that was known as the city of David that was referred to as Mount Zion. It represented that place where Yahweh dwelled and the place he reigned from as king. Mountains have a strong association with authority and being a stronghold to protect a city and reign from. A lot of times in the prophets part of the Old Testament, Zion is not referencing a physical place. In Micah 4:2 which is also echoed in Isaiah 2:3, the context is talking futuristic about a place where nations will flow into. I believe this place is a reference to Mt. Zion of the KINGDOM spiritual realm that Hebrews 12 is saying now we have access to. Isaiah and Micah were saying the time is coming when nations will flow into it and say let us go up to the mountain of the Most High. But that time is now and we can ascend the mountain of the Most High.

I also want to point out that Micah 4:2 also shows that in this mountain of the Most High, it will be a place where one will learn of his ways and walk in his paths. Then it goes on to convey that the law will come out of Mt. Zion. Mt. Zion is a place of encounter and training. It is a place to learn of his ways and know the government of the KINGDOM on another level. We have heard of the law of sin and death and the law of spirit of life but in the KINGDOM realm, there is something known as the laws of Zion. The part that says the Word shall come from Jerusalem points that also in the

KINGDOM realm, there are laws of Jerusalem. We need to ascend to Mt. Zion to engage the KINGDOM above as KINGDOM Sons.

Heavenly New Jerusalem

Mt. Zion is the holy mountain of the Lord but Jerursalem according to Micah 4:2 is the city that has the house of the Most High. This leads me to think about Matthew 5:14 when Christ said we are the light of the world and that a city that is upon a hill cannot be hidden. Mt. Zion is the holy hill and the Heavenly Jerusalem is the city linked to that hill or mountain. Abraham sought for a city which was the city of the living God. All the things of Israel were to be a picture of that which was already in heaven. It was a pattern of the atmosphere of the Most High displayed on the earth. The true promise of the Most High and his KINGDOM was not physical but it was spiritual.

8 By faith Abraham, when he was called to go out into a place which he should after receive for an __inheritance__, obeyed; and he went out, not knowing whither he went. 9 By faith he sojourned in the __land of promise__, as in a strange country, dwelling in tabernacles with Isaac and Jacob, the heirs with him of the same promise: 10 For he __looked for a city which hath foundations, whose builder and maker is God__. (Hebrews 11:8-10)

In Hebrews 11, the faith hall of fame, there in verses 8 through 10, there is a focus on Abraham. Yes, for the physical bloodline there was a land of promise but the true promise and inheritance was not the physical land. (I know some people are ready to shoot the messenger for a statement like that.) But Abraham knew this. This is why he did not settle himself in the physical land and stayed in tabernacles (tents) like he was a stranger and pilgrim. Why would he do this? Because the true promise he saw was a city which had foundations, and whose builder and maker was the Most High himself. Please stay with me on this as it is more elaborated upon later in

Hebrews 11.

*13 These **all died in faith**, **not having received the promises**, but having seen them afar off, and were persuaded of them, and embraced them, and **confessed that they were strangers and pilgrims on the earth**. 14 For they that say such things declare plainly **that they seek a country**. 15 And truly, if they had been mindful of that country from whence they came out, they might have had opportunity to have returned. 16 But now **they desire a better country**, that is, **an heavenly**: wherefore **God is not ashamed to be called their God**: for he hath **prepared for them a city**. (Hebrews 11:13-16)*

In verse 13, it goes on to say that all who were the heroes of faith , died not having received the promises because they confessed that they were strangers and pilgrims on the earth. They all plainly declared they sought a country and a city just like Abraham did. A better country they sought for than any country they could find on the earth because what they were seeking for was heavenly. But part of the new covenant where the Most High will be God and we be his people (country), he prepared for us a city. The Old Testament people did not have access to that city while they were on earth but now Christ has prepared a place for us and now we have access to this Heavenly Jerusalem.

In the Heavenly Jerusalem also known as the New Jerusalem, we walk in our true inheritance that we received by promise and faith. This is the place where the heavenly house (temple) of the Most High God is located and his throne room. As we draw nigh unto the Father , he will draw nigh unto us by revealing to us the New Jerusalem out of heaven. We see the same thing in John 14:23, Earlier in that chapter, Chris said he will go and prepare a place for us and then come back and the world won't see him but we will and he will take us where he is. So in John 14: 23, he said to those who love him and obey his commandments, that they will be loved by the Father and Christ and the Father will make their abode with him. Their abode is in heaven in the Heavenly Jerusalem and to those who qualify he will share his abode with them. Not only do we have access to Mt. Zion in the KINGDOM above, we have access now to Heavenly New Jerusalem.

Jesus Christ (Yeshua) & the Father (YHWH)

Going back to Hebrews 12 list of things we now as KINGDOM believers have access to in the KINGDOM above, the Father who is the judge of all and Christ Jesus (Yeshua) who is the mediator of the new covenant are in that list. We have access to the Father and the Son just like John 14:23 conveyed if we love them and obey the commandments of Christ Jesus (Yeshua). They will make themselves available and accessible if we continue to be faithful in our KINGDOM pursuit and be obedient.

*And **this is life eternal**, that they might **know thee the only true God, and Jesus Christ**, whom thou hast sent. (John 17:3)*

Blessed are the pure in heart for they shall see God. We have access to real face to face encounters with the Father and Son. The true KINGDOM eternal life according to John 17:3 is to know intimately the Father and the Son. In this place, we know Christ as not just King, but as elder brother and a fellow Son to the Father. In this place we do not know the Father as just the Most High King, but we know him as Father. This will be a place of true intimacy and encounter. And the Father is longing for this fellowship because the other top priority of the KINGDOM was to reconcile us back to the Father through the Son so we can be Sons.

I want to share a dream I had some years ago where I was shown a tour of the KINGDOM realm and it was presented to me in levels. One level was the level that was not even in the building which represented the lost. But the other two levels are the ones I remembered the most and saw more in detail. In the lower level, there were many in number and there was quite a busyness and there was a lot of movement and transactions if I can say it that way. This realm represented KINGDOM or ministry activity in the earth that is done by most Christians. At this level things were getting done but there was something greater.

But then my guide took me to a higher level and at this level there was stillness and peace and I was told that this was the "Abba Level" or the realm of the Father. I only saw a few people there and the few I saw would come to a main area and work together in small groups and when they were finished they would go back to their private areas. I was told this was the highest level and only a few make it because many are called but few are chosen. This represented those who would ascend in the realm of the Father (KINGDOM above) to accomplish more for the KINGDOM. I asked how do you get an invite to the higher level and I was told to go read Luke 6:35 and then the dream ended. Now is the time for KINGDOM encounter and engagement with the Father and the Son.

*But love ye your enemies, and do good, and lend, hoping for nothing again; and your **reward shall be great**, and ye shall be the **children of the Highest**: for he is kind unto the unthankful and to the evil. (Luke 6:35)*

Church of the Firstborn

*And he is the **head of the body, the church**: who is the beginning, the **firstborn from the dead**; that in all things he might have the preeminence. (Colossians 1:18)*

Christ Jesus (Yeshua) is the head (king) of the church as he is also the firstborn from the dead. The majority of people, if asked, might say the church is the physical building they go to weekly for services. Some might take it a step further and say it is the network of all believers worldwide in totality.

Another group of people might make it more exclusive and think that their denomination or sect is the only right way so the church is just talking about their group. No matter the answer, many will still be looking at the visible church that they can see on earth. But in the KINGDOM above there is a church and gathering of people that exist there.

The word "church" is the Greek word "ekklesia" which means "called out to be gathered together somewhere else". There is a scripture that says we are to come from among them and be separated. The church of the firstborn is about separation and bringing the people who abide in Christ to a gathering where worship to the Father occurs with all the citizens of heaven and the angels. It is in the realm above where it is also called "in spirit and truth". This is not about a physical location but a gathering that occurs in the heavenly temple.

In the KINGDOM now, it is not about this place or that place physically, but it is about the Father longing for those who desire to worship him to worship him in spirit and truth in the Heavenly Temple in the Heavenly Jerusalem. For the true worshippers out there, you probably have experienced this but there have been times of worship at a physical church service or even at home alone and I am aware and ascend in the realms of the Spirit and hear the angels singing and see others around the world gathering worshiping the Most High at the same time on one accord in the spirit. I put this in a perspective of worship but there are also other things that occur in the gathering and church of the firstborn. Press to not forsake the assembly of this Heavenly gathering in the KINGDOM above. Many are called but few are chosen. We must take on the KINGDOM's spiritual perspective or else there is much we will miss out on.

Angels

As you press more into the KINGDOM above, you will become more aware of the angelic hosts around you and also the ones in the higher realms of the heavens. Working with them is very important if we want to be the KINGDOM Sons that we are called to. Do you know that the angels are servants of the heirs of salvation which you are? Right now to many they are invisible to you and you have not a clue of their positioning. But as you engage the KINGDOM above, your encounter with angels will begin to increase.

There are many types and ranks of angels. Some are messenger angels that might blow shofars and also read things from proclamation scrolls. Some are warring angels carrying swords and in full battle gear. Some have wings and some don't and the Most High will use them in a plethora of ways to assist you. Some angels are angels of presence where on their arrival they fill a place with the presence of the Most High, his glory and sometimes his fire. Some angels assist in healing and so many other things. The angels hasten to perform the will of the Father and wait on your commands and decrees to assist in the advancement of the KINGDOM. Sometimes angels are bored because they are waiting on you to command them. The number of angels around the throne room is immeasurable. When you ascend into the KINGDOM above, many times it is the angels escorting you. This is another arena if you are pressing into the KINGDOM above, you will experience and engage.

Courtrooms and Councils of Heaven & the Blood

Hebrews 12 reveals the Most High as a judge of all. This is in line with the KINGDOM perspective because to be a good King you have to be able to judge well. The KINGDOM of the Most High is a government with a legal law so there are very legal aspects of the KINGDOM. If you are not aware of this, then you can end up suffering some consequences because you don't know how to maneuver legally in the KINGDOM nor understand the protocols of the Heavenly courtrooms. As there is a judicial facet in our earthly courts, there is the same in the heavenly courts of the KINGDOM above.

Now there was a day when the **sons of God came to present themselves** before the Lord, and **Satan came also among them.** (Job 1:6)

There are many terms and scriptures in the bible that point to the legality of the KINGDOM and the heavenly court rooms where the Judge of all is making judgments and decrees. I mentioned law, judge, and courts in scripture but you also have witness and testimony all throughout the scriptures. But let's look at the first chapter of the book of Job and we see a setting of a court proceeding where the Sons of God came to present themselves before the Judge of all and not only them but satan the accuser of the brethren made its way there as well. Because you have the Father who is the judge, the defendant's attorney which is Christ and then also the prosecuting attorney which is the enemy. The way to win the court case is through the new covenant, the Word of God, and the blood of the Lamb. The new covenant gives you access and benefits. The Word of God is the legal way to go against the enemy. And the blood of the Lamb has blotted out your past and the records against you and instead of speaking revenge and guiltiness like the blood of Adam, it is speaking innocence and liberty.

I want to point out that there are courts for different things. Like here on earth we have a small claims court and then there is a family court. On the international level, there are courts that judge nations and governments. The KINGDOM above does the same thing. There is a court in heaven that you go to for your personal matters. If you are interceding about a nation, city, or region, then there is a court or council for that. As a lawyer prepares for a case and has arguments and closing statements, it is good for you to prepare the same way as you approach the courts and councils of heaven.

I wish I could tell you that I am consistent in going to the courts of heaven like I should but I admit I definitely have had some success. I have had issues when it comes to family situations and financial obstacles as well that would not move for years. But then when I started to address the courts of heaven, I saw legal items in the earthly courts turn to my favor and also saw debt in the tens of thousands supernaturally erased speedily. This is also a place you can deal with generational and family curses. Because when you get in the nitty gritty of it, a lot of the things you are dealing with in life are legal loose ends that have not been addressed in the courts and councils in the KINGDOM above. Engaging these courts and councils brings you to a place of rest instead of some of the intense ways of spiritual warfare that you have been doing for years. Sometimes you have to go to court and address your accusers and put those accusations under the blood of Lamb and get that verdict and good report from the Most High. I don't have space to go into detail but press to enter into the courts and councils of heaven by faith.

Cloud of Witnesses

*1 Wherefore seeing we also are compassed about with **so great a cloud of witnesses**, let us lay aside every weight, and the sin which doth so easily beset us, and let us **run with patience the race that is set before us**, 2 Looking unto Jesus the author and finisher of our faith; who for the joy that was set before him endured the cross, despising the shame, and is **set down at the right hand of the throne of God**. (Hebrews 12:1-2)*

I will go back to the proverb that it takes a village. The goal is to get us to KINGDOM fullness as we become mature manifested Sons to all creation. We have the Holy Spirit, Christ in us, the seven spirits of God, the angels, and the Father helping us along the way in this quest. But there is even more help. They are known as the cloud of witnesses. Hebrews 12 calls them "just spirits made perfect" and another place in scripture calls them "the men in white linen". In other words, there are some people who have gone before us and already passed but have been assigned to help us on some level. I have heard some also refer to this as communion with the saints.

We are the army and the part of the team that is still present on the earth, but there is an army and part of the team doing their thing in the invisible realm of the KINGDOM above. As the first verse of Hebrews 12 shows us, we are in a race and we are also surrounded by a cloud of witnesses. We most of the time can't see them but they have an interest in how we are doing in the race because we are carrying the mantles that they once wore and they want us to fulfill the part that they didn't finish. This KINGDOM race is a relay race so we have been given the baton and we are doing our wing of the race. They are there to encourage us and sometimes to coach and instruct us.

I know this might sound crazy and strange to some and you might think I am in a place of heresy. But we see this pattern in scripture. Moses and Elijah appeared to Christ when he transfigured. We see the men in white popping up at times like at the ascension and resurrection of Christ. In the book of Revelation , John was in his heavenly vision in the spirit and he began to bow to the person next to him and was stopped immediately. It was not Christ. It was not an angel next to him, but John was told that he was a fellow servant and of his brethren the prophets. So this was a person who lived before John and was a prophet and now they are appearing to him to reveal some things to him.

Just as there are physical tribes of Israel on the earth, there are tribes when it comes to the spiritual Israel and as you engage and ascend into the KINGDOM above, you can begin to encounter your spiritual tribe and based on your spiritual lineage encounters those of old. This might happen as they appear in your room. You might see them in a dream. You might go into a spiritual trance and encounter them. You might ascend up in the councils of heaven and have a conversation. Note I am not talking about consulting with the dead and especially those who were not a part of the KINGDOM because the just spirits made perfect are not dead but they are alive unto God. With these encounters, they are on assignment from the Most High just like Elijah and Moses were when they came unto Christ. There are no limits in the KINGDOM above and for a final note, make sure you test and try the spirits by the Spirit.

Qualifications of Ascension

*3 Who shall **ascend into the hill of the Lord**? or who shall **stand in his holy place**? 4 He that hath **clean hands**, and a **pure heart**; who hath not **lifted up his soul unto vanity**, nor **sworn deceitfully**. 5 He shall receive the **blessing from the Lord**, and **righteousness from the God of his salvation. 6 This is the** generation of them that seek him, that seek thy face, O Jacob. Selah. (Psalms 24:3-6)*

I love King David because I am a part of his tribe. But more importantly, he was such a forerunner. He lived naturally under the Old Testament but was able to enjoy KINGDOM perks like someone who was in the new covenant and able to say things like don't take your Holy Spirit from me when the Holy Spirit was not given yet. As the author of the book of Psalms, in chapter 24, he to me outlines the qualifications for ascension. He starts off in verse 3 asking who will be able to ascend to the hill (mount) of the Lord which we know is Mt. Zion. And then he goes on with who will be able to stand in his holy place which is the house of the Most High in the Heavenly Jerusalem. He is not talking about a physical place because he uses the term ascend. And the generation that he sees far off is the generation that seeks him. We are, ever since Christ came, are that generation that seeks him.

And then there are listed four qualifications. And maybe to your surprise some of them point to the fact that the KINGDOM within has to be intact before you can ascend to the KINGDOM above. The four are: 1) clean hands, 2) a pure heart, 3) not lifting your soul unto vanity, and 4) not swearing deceitfully. Clean hands talk about not touching the unclean thing and coming out from among them (1 Corinthians 6:17). Having a pure heart is having a heart without a mixture that is circumcised and cleansed. A pure heart is one that operates in agape (charity) which is the God kind of love. This points to the KINGDOM within.

To not lift your soul unto vanity means to project your faith to the true and living God. Some don't believe in the Most High. Some are using idols. Some are doing meditation to try to have self awareness to nothing at all. But in Hebrews 11 it lets us know that without faith it is impossible to please God and he that comes to God must first believe that he is. We have to believe that he is and that he is real. We must then lift up our soul by ascending to him and not nothingness. And when we do that, he will be a rewarder of them that diligently seek him. Lastly we cannot swear deceitfully. We have to be sincere and not make vows out of baseless words that we don't intend to give our all to. He wants the real and the truth from your heart.

*Draw nigh to God, and **he will draw nigh to you**. **Cleanse your hands**, ye sinners; and **purify your hearts**, ye double minded. (James 4:8)*

I just wanted to add another witness from scriptures about the qualifications of ascension. In truth the word "ascension" comes from the same root that is used in the word incense which means to burn to rise. What happens when you burn an incense, the fragrance and smoke rises. We want to present ourselves as a living sacrifice so we can burn for him and ascend to him. When we look at James 4:8, we are encouraged to draw nigh unto the Most High and he will reveal himself to us. But what is interesting is that two things are given as suggestions and that is to have clean hands and a pure heart. There goes your second witness. Drawing nigh to God is to position yourself to ascend to the KINGDOM above.

Mounting Up With Wings

*But they that **wait upon the Lord** shall **renew their strength**; they shall **mount up with wings as eagles**; they shall **run**, and not be weary; and they shall **walk**, and not faint. (Isaiah 40:31)*

So we have covered on a simple level what are the qualifications of ascending to the KINGDOM above but here I want to give a key on how to ascend in a practical sense. Another favorite scripture even from my childhood is Isaiah 40:31 but I did not know of the revelation that was in this scripture. When we talk about ascending we are talking about going higher and one way to go high is flying which requires wings. This scriptures gives us a hint as to how to mount up with wings as eagles. Or should I say how to rise up on a mount (mountain) with wings like an eagle. The hint is to learn how to wait on the Most High.

I believe the reason sometimes we don't walk in the fullness of what the KINGDOM offers is because it requires time. Everyone is in a hurry and wants to pray microwave prayers when the Father is saying will you spend time with me. I can't give you an exact time it takes because there are so many factors involved and then it is relative to the person who is seeking. But to ascend you have to wait on the Lord and I will throw in as a bonus that it is better to seek him early in the morning before the day gets started and while the house is still and quiet. It is never quick to ascend into the KINGDOM above. It has always taken time. Sometimes hours of waiting. I waited for hours and nothing happened when it came to ascension. One reason for this is because he is the King and he does not move when you want him to , he draws nigh when he wants to.

There are two scriptures about being still that I love to put together. One is that we are told to be still and see the salvation of God. And the other one is to be still and know that he is God. It is through waiting and stillness that your spiritual eyes will open for you to see but also it will cause you to ascend to the place to know the Most High intimately where he is. He is a rewarder of those who diligently seek him. Like Habakkuk 2, set your watch and be still and wait and he will reveal himself and his vision so that you can run with the vision.

Something else interesting sticks out to me in Isaiah 40:31. Of course while waiting, your strength will be renewed because times of refreshing comes from the presence of the Lord. But I would have expected the progression to be , you walk, then you run, and then you fly with wings. But it starts off with mounting up with wings and then running and walking. This makes sense because you first go deeper and be still within and wait upon the Lord. Then from there you are strengthened and able to mount up with wings and ascend. So you go from deeper to higher. Then from there you come lower and forward by walking and running. After ascending higher to the KINGDOM above you, you will be in the position that allows you to then impact the things below and move the KINGDOM forward through you.

Chapter 10 : The KINGDOM Through You

*Thy **KINGDOM come**, Thy will be done **in earth, as it is in heaven**. (Matthew 6:10)*

In the previous two chapters, we discussed more about the KINGDOM within you and the KINGDOM above you. In this chapter we will discuss more in the area of the KINGDOM through you. According to the scripture above concerning the Lord's prayer shows that, the flow of the KINGDOM be-coming is from heaven (above) to the earth (below). This implies that prayer has a strong dimension to it that we as believers should engage and interface with heaven on some level and from that interchange, bring something out of heaven, to release it into the earth. In prayer there should be an interchange in the spirit to know the will of the Father as it is written and ordained above, and from there some action to align with the will that has been revealed. Prayer should not be us just asking what we want to happen but it should more so be a place where we meet with heaven and the Most High. And as conduit, we put ourselves in a position that the KINGDOM of Heaven flows THROUGH us so that the KINGDOM of God can manifest in the earth.

Our Heavenly Father is a line upon line, and precept upon precept type of God. In other words he works and reveals things in phases and stages. I know that some are just waiting for Christ to crack the sky and snap his fingers and everything be right like a little magic trick but that is not how the KINGDOM of the Most High works. The KINGDOM expands and increases strategically one territory at a time. In Matthew 13:31-33, Christ gives two parables about the KINGDOM of Heaven. In one parable, he likens the KINGDOM as taking the least of all seeds and planting it unto the tree grows to the greatest of all trees. This parable should show us that the KINGDOM is not an overnight thing but just as a tree starts with a seed and takes years to grow, the KINGDOM is no different.

In the second parable the KINGDOM is compared to leaven (yeast) where a woman HIDES it in three portions of meal till the WHOLE is leavened or risen. So the KINGDOM is a secret ingredient hidden that is set in something to eventually cause the original thing to rise and take another form. People are asking where is the KINGDOM of the Most High in the earth? Well, the KINGDOM is hidden in you and me as Christ in us is the hope of glory. We have the treasure of the KINGDOM hidden in earthen vessels , which are us, that as we go THROUGH the process of the KINGDOM, the KINGDOM can be revealed THROUGH us. There is a seed of the KINGDOM growing in you so it can be great through you. There is leaven of the KINGDOM hiding in you waiting to rise through you to conform you to the full stature and image of Christ. The KINGDOM that was hidden in appearance will not be sudden, but it will be gradual as a seed becoming a tree THROUGH the people of God.

We are looking for Christ to do all the work, but he is looking for a people who will co-partner with him as the head to manifest the KINGDOM through you. The KINGDOM of God manifesting in the earth will be through you. The flow and progression of the KINGDOM is within you to above you to through you. Another way to view it is that the trajectory is from deeper within you to higher above you to lower and forward through you. Once Christ is the King of your inner KINGDOM, then it allows you to rise for you to interface heaven, and then you will bring something lower from heaven to the earth to advance the KINGDOM forward. It is the KINGDOM's way for you to be extensions of his KINGDOM on the earth.

We are called to be ambassadors of the KINGDOM of the Most High in the earth. Ambassadors have citizenship from another land and bring a piece of their heritage to establish a relationship between their county and another country. From a KINGDOM perspective, the ambassador has been commissioned by a King to go into a territory to proclaim the decrees of the King. The ambassador has to have a close relationship with the King and also be acquainted with the palace and throne room of the King as well as be well-versed in all customs, protocols, and laws about that KINGDOM. When you begin to interact with the KINGDOM above, then you will be a sent one from the throne of the Most High with a mandate to manifest through you to the earth.

Some feel since they are prophesying and casting out devils , they are all good and flowing in the fullness of the KINGDOM. But the truth of the matter is that most of us are stuck in utilizing the GIFTS of the Spirit that comes without repentance and with no strings attached instead of walking in delegated KINGDOM authority. There is a difference. With gifts, infants in the KINGDOM can function in them and it will be as the Holy Spirit wills but delegated KINGDOM authority is for the mature Son who has let the reign of Christ in the KINGDOM within and knows the KINGDOM above on some level to have delegated power to use at their own discretion.

I want to give an example here. Working with the seven Spirits of Yahweh is greater than working with the gifts of the Holy Spirit. When it comes to the gifts, you have the word of wisdom and word of knowledge. It is just a word. It is in part. But when it comes to the seven spirits, you have the spirit of wisdom and the spirit of knowledge. A mature son has access to not just a part or a word, but has access to the fullness of wisdom and knowledge. The intention of the Most High is for the KINGDOM to rise and grow in you to mature you so that the KINGDOM can fully function through you.

Becoming Manifested Sons

*19 For **the earnest expectation** of the creature waiteth for **the manifestation of the Sons** of God. **20** For the creature was made subject to vanity, not willingly, but by reason of him who hath subjected the same in hope, **21** Because the creature itself also shall be **delivered from the bondage of corruption** into the **glorious liberty of the children of God**. **22** For we know that the **whole creation groaneth and travaileth in pain** together **until now.** (Romans 8:19-22))*

All creation is waiting with expectation for the manifestation of the mature Sons of the Most High in the earth and throughout all creation. Note it did not say earth alone but the whole of creation is groaning and looking for this manifestation. 1 John 3:2 states, "Beloved, **now are we the sons of God,** and it doth **not yet appear what we shall be**: but we know that, when **he shall appear, we shall be like him**; for we shall see him as he is." John the Revelator is saying we are the Sons of God now and to some it does not appear yet what we should be. But when Christ appears or manifests, then we shall be like him.

Some are waiting for a big universal event that is referred to as the rapture. But what if the appearing or manifesting or coming is not the rapture you've been taught to believe, but it is more of a personalized and individual appearance to those who go through the process of the KINGDOM. John

14:21-23 and the whole chapter as a matter of fact, talks about the appearance of Christ to those who love him and obey his commandments to them individually where the rest of the world won't see him but they will. Then it continues in verse 23 to say that by your obedience to the King you will be loved by Christ and the Father and they will manifest themselves to you and make their abode with you. It is in this moment as you overcome, that Christ will appear in such a way with the Father and you will be transformed and change into the same image of Christ to become a manifested son of the Most High..

You will be a son because now you know the Father in a real way. Without holiness, no man can see the Father. Blessed are the pure in the heart for they shall see God the Father. I know this may be some heavy stuff to swallow and I am probably rattling some theological cages at the moment but the truth is the Most High is calling for you now to overcome and become manifested Sons of the KINGDOM now. In this, the KINGDOM will flow through you into the earth and all creation. It is not his first choice for you to wait till you die to enjoy aspects of heaven. But his first intention is the pattern of the first Adam that you through the cross of Christ enter into the KINGDOM and bear the image of the Son to have dominion on the earth while you are here. He wants you to be a mature KINGDOM Son who overcomes and walks in their inheritance now, which is the KINGDOM through you.

The inheritance is not just for any child of the KINGDOM. In Romans 8, "sons" is actually the Greek word "huios" which means mature male son in contrast to Greek word "teknon" which means a child (either son or daughter). Sometimes in the gospels Christ is preaching sonship but it was translated into children instead of sons. Like when Christ says blessed are the peacemakers for they shall be called the "children" of God. That should say they should be called the "sons" of God. In the first chapter of the Gospel of John, the purpose of Christ coming was to give mankind power to become Sons of the Most High. To inherit the KINGDOM you have to become a son who is conformed to the image of Christ. In this the Father can grant you the authority of the KINGDOM so that through you corruption and bondage can be removed in the earth and all creation.

Kings and Priests (Melchizedek) To Bless the Earth

*18 And **Melchizedek king of Salem** brought forth **bread and wine**: and he was the priest of the most high God. 19 And **he blessed him**, and **said, Blessed be Abram of the most high God**, **possessor of heaven and earth**: 20 And blessed be the most high God, which hath delivered thine enemies into thy hand. And he gave him tithes of all. (Genesis 14:18-20)*

There are different spellings of Melchizedek in the Old Testament than in the New Testament of the bible. But Melchizedek means "king of righteousness". In the scripture of this section (Genesis 14) it shows Melchizedek as the king of Salem which means "peace" and then it proclaims that he is a priest of the Most High God. Also, from Psalms and the book of Hebrews we see that Christ is a priest of the order of Melchizedek so they both are part of the same priesthood. This Melchizedek also existed before Moses and the Levitical priesthood was initiated in the earth. So the order of Melchizedek is a king-priest hybrid royal priesthood that is an eternal order that we are called to through Christ.

1 Peter 2 lets us know that we are a "royal priesthood" and Revelation 1 shares with us that we have been made kings and priests. I also like the fact that one scripture elaborates that the KINGDOM of God is righteousness, peace and joy in the Holy Ghost. So it is interesting that Melchizedek is a king of righteousness who reigns over a city of peace called "Salem" which is the suffix part of the city JeruSALEM. So we have the mixture of righteousness and peace with a king in this Melchizedek person. This combination points to something that is aligned with the KINGDOM of the Most High. Not only that, Melchizedek, the king-priest, also was used to "bless" Abraham

while serving bread and wine (communion). This is an interesting picture.

And now with Christ, we see that Christ is re-establishing the priesthood after the order of Melchizedek in the earth while doing away with the Levitical priesthood. Melchizedek here in Genesis 14 is present before Moses and Solomon have established any tabernacle or temple. So if Melchizedek was a priest, what temple did he operate in? Could it be that he functioned in a heavenly temple in a heavenly JeruSALEM that manifested in the earth to bring heaven to earth as a pattern of what the Most High wanted out of us? When Melchizedek blessed Abram, he declared that he was the possessor (inheritor) of heaven and earth. Isn't the blessing over Abram, the intention of the KINGDOM of the Most High that he gave to the first Adam that we as mankind be the possessor of heaven and earth? I hope you are seeing these same parallels and correlations.

The order and royal priesthood we are called to is one where we reign as kings from above to impact and bless the earth. There are thrones above with your name on it ready for you to sit on. From there, you are given the scepter and the keys of the KINGDOM so you can decree justice, judgments, liberty, and newness. From the priest's perspective, once you fully function as the temple of the Holy Ghost in your body, you will ascend to give service in the heavenly and holy temple above where you can be a mediator before the Most High and the earth. Here you can worship the Most High in spirit and truth and as a priest provide service and also navigate in the courts and councils of the KINGDOM above. There will be much to learn while navigating in the KINGDOM above and of course the aspect of the priest is linked to having holiness to the Most High.

I want to note that the role of Melchizedek's kings and priests is behind the scenes most of the time because it is done in the spiritual realm and in the KINGDOM above. The identification of people who have reached this level in the KINGDOM is that they don't see themselves as just physical men and women born in the flesh but their identification is with Christ. They see themselves as born again spirit beings that have no ancestry or genealogy of the flesh. A lot of what is done in this order is done in secret and what you do in secret will be rewarded openly by the Father. This service or priesthood is done in the KINGDOM above without observation of the natural eyes. But the KINGDOM through you brings manifestation for eyes to see.

One last thing I want to hit in this section is that the job of the King-priest role is to bless people and all creation. The KINGDOM within you combined with the KINGDOM above now will put you in position to be authorized by the Most High as a mature son to bring transformation and blessing to the earth as the KINGDOM works through you as a mediator. You will literally stand in the gap to be the conduit of the flow from the KINGDOM above to the KINGDOM of God on earth. This blessing will be initiated by us just like Melchizedek blessed Abram with his words. The true kings and priests after the order of Melchizedek through Christ are a new creation that brings change everywhere they go and declare. Being a king and priest is for the purpose that the KINGDOM can flow through you.

Called To Influence and Fill the Earth With KINGDOM

The high calling of the KINGDOM through you is for you to influence and fill (replenish) the earth. Remember, the KINGDOM of the Most High is the King in you, above you, and through you for the intent of being all in all. He wants to fill all the empty places with Him. He desires to fill the dry places with his living water. By his living bread, he wants to feed the hungry and poor and it is his will to cover every place that is saturated in darkness with light. He wants to do all this through you.

In the beginning on the seventh day the Father rested. Then Christ came, died, rose again, and ascended to the right hand of the Father to rest. Christ is the head and we are the body. We are his extension on the earth. So then the Holy Spirit was sent to be poured out upon all flesh, especially the body of Christ. Why? Because we got next and that next is now. It was to empower us to become sons of God and to continue the growth of the KINGDOM throughout all creation. He wants to flow the KINGDOM through you.

Staying with the body analogy, Christ is the head which means he sends signals to his body to carry out his purpose. It would be strange if all you saw was a head walking around with no neck or the rest of the body with the expectation to function like a full body and get things done. That would be ludicrous to think that would be possible. It is the same thing with the Most High and Christ. He designed us to be his body so we can help and carry out the KINGDOM Agena. And with us being the body, we are different in every way. Some of us are necks. Some of us are the hands and fingers. Others are the legs and feet. Some are the heart of the body. And I can go on and on. I have said this to say we are not all the same and the way the KINGDOM flows through us will be unique to every single person.

Not everyone is called to preach in a pulpit. Not everyone is called to teach the Word of God. Not everyone is called to be an international missionary that goes to many countries. Some are called to work in their jobs. Some are called to be excellent mothers and fathers. Some are called to be government officials and CEOs that influence the government and bless the marketplace. The KINGDOM through us, because there is no limit to the Most High, has endless possibilities and roles.

In one of my books, *Testimony Scrolls of Destiny: The Overcomer's Secret Weapon,* I talk about how before we came to the earth we were given a scroll with a mandate that was customized just for us and how we need to find and uncover that scroll to fulfill our destiny. Between the KINGDOM within and the KINGDOM above, we should begin to figure out what is the mandate and commission on our lives from the King. And different mandates because they are for certain seasons might not be revealed until certain points in our journey. Some things are not clear because we are not entering the

KINGDOM within and the KINGDOM above so we can receive the scroll and mandate so that the KINGDOM can now be through us. We need to walk out our part as a member of the body. Christ is a multi membered body. The substance of the body is no different than the head. The vine is not a different substance than the branches. It has the same DNA. As we align to Christ, we are a part of Christ.

*And the seventh angel sounded; and there were great voices in heaven, saying, **The KINGDOMS of this world are become the KINGDOMS of our Lord, and of his Christ;** and he shall reign for ever and ever. (Revelation 11:5)*

The goal of the KINGDOM is to be all in all. In the earth whatever you want to consider a KINGDOM or a realm of influence, Christ and the Father wants to invade. And guess who he wants to use to do this? You guessed it. It is you.

I mentioned in a previous chapter that there was a movement started in 1975 by evangelicals Loren Cunningham, Bill Bright, and Francis Schaeffer called the Seven Mountain Mandate. It holds that there are seven aspects of society that believers should seek to influence:

1. Family
2. Religion
3. Education
4. Media
5. Entertainment
6. Business
7. Government

Now I can't say I totally agree with the movement or even the seven spheres of influence they named. But at a high level I agree this is similar to the notion of a KINGDOM flowing through you. The Most High wants to flow the KINGDOM through you to invade, reign, and influence every territory you can imagine that is on this earth. Yes, husbands and wives should reign in their families. Some should make their impact in the religion aspect of the KINGDOM. And the same follows with areas like education, media, entertainment, business, and government. The KINGDOM of the Most High should be taking the lead through you in these areas.

We can't limit the KINGDOM of the Most High to just the religious arena but the KINGDOM needs to extend out of the walls of the church and make an impact where there is KINGDOM penetration in every area. This type of movement in KINGDOM believers will cause the Most High to be all in all through us. Not all will be the Elijahs, Moseses, Samuels, Pauls, Johns, and Peters. But some will be Josephs and Daniels who found favor and influence in government and business. Know that you are called to a domain and that domain might be just your family or community for the moment. Or it might be to be a pastor or be president of the United States. When you have clarity of what your KINGDOM mandate is, go and replenish that part of the earth you have been given authority and dominion over. Let the KINGDOM flow through you to the ends of the earth and all creation.

Saviors on the Mount

*And **saviours shall come up on mount Zion** to judge the mount of Esau; and **the KINGDOM shall be the Lord's**. (Obadiah 1:21)*

We that are in the KINGDOM of the Most High need to be conformed to the image and likeness of the first begotten Son in every way. He is the pattern and we need to follow that pattern. We have thought about ourselves as kings under the King of Kings. We are called to be priests as he is our High Priest. We are lords as he is the Lord of Lords. He is the Branch that is from the stem of Jesse, and we are branches of his vine. We can continue this logic for a while. But in this section, I want to key in that Christ is a savior and we are called to be saviors as well.

A savior from the Hebrew word "yasa" means to free, to defend, to deliver, to help, to preserve, to rescue and to achieve victory. As Christ has overcome the enemy, the world, and death, we are called to overcome as well. Why? Just so we can say that we have victory and our sins have been forgiven. No. It is more than that because as he is , so are we in this present world. Christ has made us free from the curse. Per the scripture of this section, we have to be in position from Mount Zion to be able to be saviors or manifested Sons to the earth. He has defended us in the courts of heaven to secure the not guilty verdict. The Holy Spirit , the comforter and helper, has been sent to help us. And we for sure have been rescued from the miry clay and horrible pit to secure salvation from our King and Savior. We are called to be saviors as well as we allow the KINGDOM to flow through us.

Note that in Obadiah 1:21, the word "saviors" is plural. It is not one savior but there are many as Christ is a many membered body. It is Christ and those in Christ who are kings, priests, lords, mature sons, and also saviors. Another thing to notice is where the saviors are positioned. The saviors are upon Mt. Zion. We need to ascend high into the KINGDOM above and overcome to stand on Mt. Zion to be the saviors to bring salvation to the rest of the world.

*18 The Spirit of the Lord is upon me, because **he hath anointed me** to preach the gospel to the poor; he hath sent me to heal the brokenhearted, to preach deliverance to the captives, and recovering of sight to the blind, to set at liberty them that are bruised, 19 To preach the acceptable year of the Lord. (Luke 4:18-19)*

The word "Christ" means the anointed one who brings salvation or let's say an "anointed savior". As we are a part of the body of Christ, we are also anointed saviors as well. As Christ Jesus (Yeshua) is anointed to preach, heal, deliver, recover, and bring liberty and salvation, so are we. We are called to be saviors. As we rise to the KINGDOM above, we can have a right standing on Mt. Zion to proclaim blessing from a position of high authority into the earth. Psalms 133 shows that the blessing flows from top to bottom as the oil goes from the head to the beard and to the skirts and below. With the head of the KINGDOM being above, the KINGDOM flows through his body to the earth which is his footstool. We are the body of Christ (saviors) where the KINGDOM will flow through us to transform and bring blessing to the earth and all creation.

Invisible to Visible, Inner To Outer, Above To Below

The KINGDOM through us does so many things to transform creation. Once again to many, the Father is invisible. Christ said he will appear to the place where some will see him where others will not. And that he will have to manifest himself to those who qualify. The KINGDOM is without observation and not of this world. So as the KINGDOM flows through you, the things that were invisible become visible. Not only do you see the invisible by faith but that which is ordained above, becomes visible or manifests through you. So the KINGDOM through you brings that which is invisible into the visible plane on earth.

Also besides manifesting that which was once invisible, the KINGDOM through us brings that which is in the KINGDOM within us to the outer. The way of the KINGDOM inside us is for him to fill your heart, mind, and soul with a renewed spirit so that your new nature will show through your works of love to people and your obedience to the Most High. The KINGDOM within will have rivers of living water that will flow from inside to out and overflow into everything around you.

Lastly, the KINGDOM flows through you from above to below which causes you to move the KINGDOM's agenda forward. It is easy for us to get caught up in ourselves and our lives around us, but creation is so much bigger and vast. Have you ever heard of that person who is 50 years old and they never left their hometown? That is all they know. Or better yet, have you ever seen someone who is an immigrant in one country and for decades has never been back to their homeland? They have acclimated more to the country they immigrated and forget from whence they came. That is how the Father views some of us and he is saying come back home in the KINGDOM above. We must seek those things above and let our affections be towards the things above so we can propagate heaven to earth. We want to live in a new reality where we can say it is like heaven on earth. This is the dream of the Father where we are the main characters of the dream that is manifesting heaven and the KINGDOM above to be the KINGDOM of God on the earth.

New Heaven New Earth

Nevertheless we, **according to his promise, look for new heavens and a new earth**, wherein **dwelleth righteousness**. (2 Peter 3:13)

Once again, the KINGDOM of heaven is like a seed that was planted and now growing to be the greatest tree where fowls of the air can lodge in. In other words, the growth and expansion of the KINGDOM happens gradually. The promise of the Most High is that there will be new heavens and a new earth. This takes us back to the beginning of Genesis 1:1 that in the beginning God created the heavens and the earth. Notice heavens is plural because there are levels to the KINGDOM above. But the heavens were corrupted by the angels' rebellion and the earth cursed because of the fall of Adam. So the goal was to get us back to the way he intended in the beginning concerning the heavens and earth.

The new heavens and earth is where righteousness dwells. The KINGDOM of the Most High is righteousness, joy, and peace. The Melchizedek order is kings and priests of righteousness. The KINGDOM exists under new heavens and with a new earth. The KINGDOM within is there because something new happens in the heavens. Access to the KINGDOM above is available because the prince of the power of the air has been defeated and the heavens is new in a way that it was before.

Some are waiting for it all to happen at one time where you blink and the new heavens and new earth is there. This is not how the KINGDOM works. It is gradual and must go through a certain sequence. There cannot be a new earth without there being new heavens because flow has to be from above to below. The earth was created to be an expression and extension of the heavens. Did you notice that the Father created the things above before he created the things below? It is the pattern of creation and the KINGDOM to flow in that way.

The transition of the new heavens and new earth has already started. The work of Christ on the cross was so powerful that he was able to say, "It is finished". With Calvary, he set something in motion. He set in motion the KINGDOM of the Most to take over from above to below and to advance from the headquarters of the KINGDOM out to the outskirts of creation. Did you hear when he died, he overcame the enemy and death and the grave could not hold him? Then after that, he resurrected and then ascended to the Father and now sits at the right hand of the Father. Maybe you heard that he spoiled principalities and powers and now flows in dominion and has been given a name that is greater than any other name. What am I trying to say? I am saying that the heavens are new and continue to be made new.

And it is because the heavens are new and being renewed, we have access now to ascend higher to sit on empty thrones after we dethrone whatever else he is trying to sit on our thrones. We sit together with Christ in heavenly places. We have to press and make that our living reality where we are aware that this is our position. Someone might say "The heavens are new and continue to be new through you." As we ascend and acknowledge our new position and authority, then we make the heavens new day by day. And because of that, we now have the power to make earth new day by day.

We are to go and occupy the heavens and bring part of the heavens down to make a new earth. We are to be fruitful and replenish the earth to new. If you are a new creation and the Father is doing a new thing, then you can ascend into the new heavens and transform this world into a new earth. The reason why we are not seeing what we want to see is because some believers are ignorant of the KINGDOM gameplan. Others know the game plan but not playing to those rules. And some are trying and losing the battle. When we come to a place to overcome the enemy and continue to press for that which we were created, then we can see the change. See now, there are a few here and there. But when the numbers grow and the saints really get the revelation and begin to truly enter in, look out because more of the KINGDOM will manifest and become visible on the earth. Christ is looking for his church to be glorious as the KINGDOM flows through them on the earth.

Breath and Authority

And the earth was without form, and void; and darkness was upon the face of the deep. **And the Spirit (breath) of God** moved upon the face of the waters. (Genesis 1:2)

And the Lord God formed man of the dust of the ground, and **breathed into his nostrils the breath of life**; and man became a living soul. (Genesis 2:7)

In the final part of this chapter, I want to discuss the importance of breath and how it has a connection to power and authority. Any word that you look up in the Greek or the Hebrew that is translated "spirit", it will also have "breath" as another meaning. And you will see this vice versa when you look up the word "breath" in the Greek or Hebrew. The Holy Spirit can also be known as the Holy Breath.

In Genesis 1:2, there was void and darkness and it took the Spirit (breath) of God to move upon it to bring transformation and change. Then in Genesis 2:7, for man to become a living soul with an alive spirit, the Most High had to breathe into man to bring life. Breath is very powerful because it originated from the Father. After , the breath hovered over the waters in Genesis 1:2, then the Most High extended his breath through his words and decreed, "Let there be light". When you release words, you are releasing breath. That is why Christ said my words are spirit (breath) and life. If the breath (words) released are not aligned to the Father who is the originator, then that breath turns from being life to death. Hence, life and death is in the power of the tongue.

21 Then said Jesus to them again, Peace be unto you: as my Father hath sent me, even so send I you. **22** And when he had said this, **he breathed on them**, and saith unto them, **Receive ye the Holy Ghost: 23 Whose soever sins ye remit, they are remitted unto them; and whose soever sins ye retain, they are retained**. (John 20:21-23)

That is why after Christ resurrected and before the day of Pentecost in John 20, he had to do something similar that the Most High did in the beginning, and breathe on the disciples. It is the breathing of Christ here that made them born again and no longer beings of the fallen nature but conceived by the breath of Christ. And after Christ breathed on them, he kept the breath going through his words and let them know that after he breathed on them, they now walked in another level of authority. They received his breath that in turn transformed their breath to contain the power and authority to remit and retain sins. The first Adam was a living soul, but the second Adam

(Christ) is a quickening, making alive spirit. So when we receive the breath of the Holy Ghost , we are made alive because his words and breath are life.

The breath is contagious in a sense. Just like if someone has a cold or flu and they hang around someone else, then that person is susceptible to get that cold or flu. Why? Because they were breathing the same air and breath. So if we are receiving the breath of the Holy Spirit, then we are in the position to breathe out the same breath and everything that is contained in that breath. If we breathed in power and authority, then we are now new creations to do as Christ did to us to others. Now I am not saying to go around breathing on people but I am saying your breath and your words have power. Let everything that has breath, his breath, praise the LORD.

This is why it is important to let the KINGDOM reign within you to eventually get your tongue aligned with the KINGDOM. And this is why it is important to ascend into the realms of the KINGDOM above, so that now you can speak that which you heard on high down below. It is from above that you will receive delegated and mandated power. Christ was able to say that he only did and said what he heard and saw the Father do.

Through faith we understand that the **worlds were framed by the word of God**, so that **things which are seen were not made of things which do appear**. (Hebrews 11:3)

We have to follow the example of Christ and the Father who used their breath and words to release their power of life and transformation. We have that same breath because of the Holy Spirit. In Hebrews 11:3, we see that the worlds were framed by the Word (breath) of the Most High. He spoke (breathed) and it became. But the next part of the scripture I love is where it shows that anything that is visible or seen was and is made by things that we don't see physically. Let me say it another way. Everything we see in the physical has an origin from something that is spiritual.

You don't like what you see in your life, then let's check for the source. Now that we are KINGDOM Sons, we have the power to frame the worlds of creation. Because of his breath, we can release our breath of authority through our words to declare that which is above in the heavens to appear down below in the earth. We can breathe out words of life to make the earth a living and new earth. Seek to get in the position where the KINGDOM flows from above through you to below to forward the KINGDOM of God on the earth.

Chapter 11 : KINGDOM Weapons To Help You Overcome

*He that **overcometh** shall **inherit all things;** and **I will be his God**, and **he shall be my son.** (Revelation 21:7)*

We are to seek, see, enter, inherit, and enlarge the KINGDOM of the Most High. But in this chapter, I wanted to give focus to how to overcome and how that relates to inheriting the KINGDOM. To inherit the KINGDOM of God, you have to overcome something. The fact that one scriptures says that to enter the KINGDOM comes with much tribulation shows that there is an obstacle there. Another scripture states that you have to press and take the KINGDOM by force. This infers there is an enemy present. To overcome means to come to something and overtake it. All this language and verbiage links to the fact that we are in a war. In this war, he does not want us to inherit just a piece of it but he wants us to inherit and possess it all. He wants us to have the same mentality and intention he has where we like him, want it all. He wants to be all in all and he wants us to inherit all things through the vehicle of overcoming in war.

To be honest, writing this book has come with a lot of warfare. While writing this chapter, which I originally wrote to be chapter 5, as well as chapter 4, I was stuck for months without writing. (After much consideration with my inner circle, it was recommended to have this chapter near the end of the book.) I believe the delay was because the Lord wanted to show me more concerning this chapter and the one before. Also because I was writing about warfare, the enemy wanted to give me warfare.

Best believe that when you receive revelation or meditate on the Word of God, you will be tested in it. Remember the principle with every word of revelation that the enemy will come immediately to steal it away from you. But as I was praying specifically for a release and declaring that this book will be finished according to my KINGDOM assignment, that night I had a dream. And the dream came with such an anointing that all delay that was there before was washed away with a spirit of acceleration. And I literally wrote chapter 4 in one day. And the flow of this chapter poured out of me as well. (I felt the presence of God very strongly as I wrote the last two paragraphs.)

Dream

The dream I had was where I was fighting against the enemy and this goat. My goal was I had to capture the goat. They needed someone to fight and I volunteered. There was a crowd watching. It seemed like I was the underdog. I was bold and had no fear. At first I tried to fight the enemy and take the goat by force with physical strength. Eventually a voice came out of the wall that I think I could only hear and it was God reminding me that in the law of Moses that using goats for sacrifices became outdated as the enemy was defeated by Christ and his blood. In my own strength, the goat was biting and hurting my hand but when I began to stand and declare the Word of

God with faith and boldness , the power and glory of God rose from within. I could see the light of the glory and it grew eventually to be outside of me and defeated the enemy and the goat. The crowd cheered and I yelled with victory as I pumped my fist up in the air. While doing this the dream ended and I woke up to hear the Holy Spirit talking to me about the dream.

I was told that the dream represented me defeating the enemy and his law (religion and tradition) with faith, the Holy Spirit, and the Word of God. As the word of God was being declared about the power of Christ and his blood, the enemy and his weaponry was defeated and destroyed. There was a showdown, a battle and a war. But with the right weapons, I overcame the enemy and the other things connected to him. But I could not do it in my strength but needed God's word and his spirit. The Holy Spirit continued and concluded to talk to me about the four main things that the Word shows us we need to overcome. Let's discuss as we progress in this chapter what they are and how to overcome them. They are the following:

- The enemy
- The world
- The flesh
- The law

Overcoming the Enemy

And they overcame him by the **blood of the Lamb**, and by t**he word** of their testimony; and they **loved not their lives unto the death**. (Revelation 12:11)

In the flow of discussion about believers being KINGDOM overcomers, the first opponent that we will put focus on is the adversary himself. He is known as the devil, that old serpent, and satan. He is the pinnacle of the KINGDOM in darkness who has a network of agents under him and a system to bring destruction in our lives if we let him. But I am here in this book to let you know that we are more than conquerors against the enemy through Christ.

The aforementioned scripture being Revelation 12:11 points out that there are three things that the Most High have gifted the believer with to defeat the enemy himself. We have been given the blood of the Lamb, the Word of God, and the lack of fear through love.

The Weapon of The Blood of the Lamb

We have heard the saints say, "there is power in the blood" and this is such a true statement. The blood is so powerful because the blood sacrifice of Christ has given us access to the KINGDOM of God. It has also blotted out the record against us and made and declared us as righteous. See, the enemy is the accuser of the brethren and he goes along trying to talk about your past and your shortcomings. It is the blood of Christ that speaks even in the courts of heaven to declare that you are in covenant with the Most High and you are off limits to the enemy.

But you have to have faith in the blood of the Lamb. From experience, time after time, I have seen the power of the blood of the Lamb and make sure everyday with a heart of repentance , I plead or apply the blood of the Lamb against the enemy.

Over 25 years ago, one night I woke up out of my sleep and my eyes and ears were opened up to the spiritual realm. I heard this sound of dissonance like you would hear in a horror movie. Along with this sound, I heard these very evil laughs and cackles and the sound of little pitter patters of feet all around me. I began then to see little imp demons that look like jesters or the beings you will see on a Joker's card in a deck of cards. Dressed in the colors of green, red, and white, they started to taunt me with the words of "We are going to kill you." There were even some that were walking on my ceiling upside down.

Shockingly enough, I was not fearful. I instantly yelled out, "Leave in the name of Jesus". And what happened next shocked me. A red cloud of liquidly substance appeared on the scene starting from the ceiling and moved around the room. As it moved around the bedroom, the imp demons left with the quickness. This was when I realized first hand in a very vivid experience, the power of the blood of the Lamb along with the name of Jesus. The blood of the Lamb is no doubt beneficial in the war against the enemy.

The Weapon of the Word of God

*For the **word of God is quick, and powerful, and sharper than any twoedged sword**, piercing even to the dividing asunder of soul and spirit, and of the joints and marrow, and is a discerner of the thoughts and intents of the heart. (Hebrews 4:12)*

The next weapon to defeat and overcome the enemy in conjunction with the blood of the Lamb is the Word of God. In Ephesian 6, when the pieces of the full armor of God are mentioned, the sword of the Spirit is listed. And out of all the armor of God , the sword is the obvious offensive weapon to attack with. You might be thinking why are we talking about the sword of the Spirit when this section is supposed to be about the Word of God being a weapon? The answer is because Ephesians 6:17 declares that the sword of the Spirit is the same thing as the Word of God. And the aforementioned scripture of Hebrews 4:12 highlights that the Word of God is very much alive (quick), powerful, and sharp like a sword.

In another place in the bible, the Messiah declares that his "words" are spirit and life. The Word from the beginning and the Word that was with God and was God is a weapon that we can use. Christ is the Word of God and if he lives in you , you have a weapon. We are not just talking about words being powerful but the Word of God is powerful. We are not talking about a carnal and worldly weapon but the spiritual weapon of the Word of God because his "words" are spirit and life. It is so powerful that it can displace death and establish life.

What I believe is interesting is that in the new testament you have two Greek words for "word". One is the Greek word "logos" and the Greek word "rhema". They are both similar in that they mean a word uttered by a living voice. But "logos" represents a general word that embodies a concept or idea. Whereas, "rhema" represents a series of words that makes a declaration of one's mind.

Now when we look at Hebrews 4:12 and Ephesians 6:17, even though it mentions "the word" being like a sword, they use two different Greek words. Hebrews 4:12 uses the logos Word and Ephesians 6:17 uses the rhema Word. I believe the tie into "logos" and "rhema" is that the "logos" is that which has been spoken, declared, and established by God Almighty. But the "rhema" Word is that alive word that is birthed in our hearts and mind that we speak and declare that aligns with the "logos" word. You don't have "rhema" without first having "logos" first established.

It is not just the "logos" Word that gets the job done from Revelation 12:11 where it says that they overcame the enemy by the word of their "testimony". The "word" in that scripture is "logos". But it needs "testimony". It is the testimony or expressed witness of the "logos" inside that becomes a sword to pierce and devour the enemy every time. We need the converted "logos" word that becomes the "rhema" word when released as a testimony and weapon of catastrophic consequences to the KINGDOM in darkness.

*This **book of the law shall not depart out of thy mouth**; but thou **shalt meditate therein day and night**, that thou **mayest observe to do according to all that is written therein**: for then thou shalt make thy way prosperous, and* *then thou shalt have good success. (Joshua 1:8)*

The process of transforming the "logos" Word to the "rhema" Word is meditation of the Word. In other words, the "logos" Word of God must be digested in a way that the Word is written in your hearts and mind so it can then be released as "rhema" Word out of your mouth. To meditate on the general or written Word of God is to ponder or speak to yourselves so much till the Word becomes a part of you and alive in you. When this happens you begin to speak the "rhema" Word and act upon the "rhema" Word. This will make your way prosperous and full of success against the enemy. All the enemy can do with the Word is try to warp and pervert it. But when the truth of the Word as a sword is pierced into the enemy, he must retreat and you will be made free. The truth shall make you free.

As an example, we see the Messiah our Christ after he was baptized by John the Baptist. He is led into the wilderness by the Holy Spirit to be tempted by the enemy. The enemy shows with a series of tests to tempt him in the area of hunger, lust, pride, and fame but each time the Messiah would hit the enemy with the Word of God. Without fail for every temptation, Christ would declare, "It is written". Christ was already in a mode of prayer and fasting. He has been baptized by the Holy Spirit but he needed the Word of God to defeat the enemy. After this battle in the KINGDOM war, the enemy had to retreat and wait for an opportune time to try again. The Word of God living in us and being declared through us is an unstoppable KINGDOM weapon to overcome the enemy.

The Weapon of Love For The Most High

And they overcame him by the blood of the Lamb, and by the word of their testimony; and they **loved not their lives unto the death**. (Revelation 12:11)

The third KINGDOM weapon implied in Revelation 12:11 concerning

177

overcoming the enemy is the love we have for the Most High. It states that they loved not love their lives even unto death. In other words, their love for the Most High was greater than their love for love for themselves. These align with the first and greatest commandment per Christ which is to love the Lord our God with all our heart, mind, soul, and strength. Then Christ also adds that to love him is to obey his commandments. So with our love for the Most High comes full obedience no matter how we are tempted even if death would be our portion.

> *There is no fear in love; but perfect love casteth out fear: because fear hath torment. He that feareth is not made perfect in love. (1 John 4:18)*

When fear of death is taken out of the equation, then what can the enemy throw your way? When fear of what your reputation is and what people might say is non-existent, the impact of the blows of the enemy is lessened greatly. 1 John 4:18 declares that perfect love casts out fear. When fear is present , then torment from the enemy has an opening to appear and do its thing. But if our love and obedience for the Most High is all that matters and it is unwavering, we will overcome the enemy every time. The Most High has not given us the spirit of fear , but that of power, love and a sound mind. Where fear is absent, power to overcome the enemy is present and enabled. Steadfast love and obedience to our living God is a KINGDOM weapon to overcome the enemy.

Overcoming The World

> *For **whatsoever is born of God** overcometh the world: and this is the victory that overcometh the world, **even our faith**. (1 John 5:4)*

In this KINGDOM war, we know now we have to defeat the enemy. He is the source of opposition to the KINGDOM of God and he is the father of lies. But we need to understand that he alone was not enough in his eyes to be a worthy opponent. He needed a system and infrastructure to infuse his plans and strategies into for the purpose of implementing his bidding. This system, network, illusion or facade is "the world". It is like Apple having apps and programs but it needs an operating system within a piece of hardware. The enemy has an "operating system" layer that he is installing his programs to run in and on top of the earth that was created originally for God's glory.

There is a world that God intended and one that the enemy wants to propagate. One scripture says that the enemy is the "god" (lowercase "g") of this world. But another place in the bible lets us know that the earth is the Lord's and the fullness thereof. The earth is what God intended for his KINGDOM to be established and gave the charge to mankind to have dominion and replenish the earth but while we slept in our slumber, ignorance, and disobedience, the enemy has chosen to plant a world system in the earth.

*For **all that is in the world**, the **lust of the flesh**, and **the lust of the eyes**, and the **pride of life,** is not of the Father, but is of the world. (1 John 2:16)*

This world system as the previous scripture in 1 John shows, has the agenda to trigger mankind in three ways. The first way is the lust of the flesh. The world system will put before us that which appeals to our five senses. The second way is through the lust of the eye which shows the importance of the eye since it is the window of the soul. When the eye is single, focused and filled with light, it impacts the rest of the body. So of course, the enemy really wants to entice your eye gates. The lust of the flesh and the lust of the eye work hand in hand.

And thirdly, the enemy and his world system wants to appeal to the area of pride within you which causes you to walk in a carnal life instead of a spiritual life. When the focus is on you, your life will be selfish and carnal. But when the focus is on the Most High, our life will be spiritual, being filled with victory and love. These are the same tests that the first Adam failed when he was in the garden of Eden. But the second Adam passed these same tests in the wilderness to pave the way for us. We are called to overcome these aspects and tuggings that are a part of the enemy's world system.

In the Greek of the New Testament, you have a word for "earth" but then two Greek words are being used for "world". One word is "kosmos" which means the entirety of the earth, the universe and its government. The other word is "aion" which really does not mean "world" but more so an age with a duration of time and rule. So when the enemy is referred to as the "god" of this world, it is the Greek word "aion" that hints to a temporal duration of time or age where a system is in place. This "world" system is what we see with our natural eyes everyday that has a spiritual backing of the enemy. In our quest to be mature Sons of the KINGDOM of God, we must use the right KINGDOM weapons to overcome the world system of the enemy.

The Weapon of Being Born Again

*Jesus answered and said unto him, Verily, verily, I say unto thee, Except a man **be born again**, he cannot **see the KINGDOM of God**. (John 3:3)*

The "world" that the enemy is projecting is an illusion full of lies. And the best way to overcome this world is to change what we see. We have to come to the realization that we have two sets of eyes. During the fall of Adam and Eve (Genesis 3), when they ate of the fruit of the forbidden tree, the bible let us know that their eyes were opened. Which eyes were opened? Their physical eyes were open. We knew that they could see before the fall because they were using their spiritual eyes and could see the garden and the trees. I believe what happened when their physical eyes were opened, then their spiritual eyes were closed, their glory and fire of their spirit man was extinguished, and they saw from a perspective of their own reasonings and what the enemy wanted them to see.

This warped sight and vision that befell Adam and Eve was passed down to the generations following where we were living in the illusion world of the enemy. We were operating in his system and rules. But thanks be to the Almighty God who sent his Son, the living Christ, so we can be born again. After the fall, there was definitely a need for us being born again which is why Christ is called the second Adam. This is why Christ declared in the scripture listed in John 3 that to "see" the KINGDOM, you must be born again. And later he lets us know that to be born again , it must be by his Spirit and by water.

That word "Spirit" also means his "breath". The first Adam is a living soul, but the second Adam (Christ) is a quickening (making alive) spirit. In Genesis, for the first Adam to become a living soul, God the Father had to breathe in the nostrils of Adam for him to become living. After the fall, because he ate from the wrong tree, he surely died. And because the first Adam needed breath (the spirit) to become alive, then for the second Adam to make us alive again (born again), it had to be by breath or his Spirit as well. This is why in John 20:20, Christ after his resurrection appeared before the disciples and told them to receive the Holy Spirit while he "breathed" on them. This is the point where they became "born again" and the new spirit man was conceived. This was before the day of Pentecost when they were baptized by the Holy Ghost and filled with God's spirit.

So in a fallen state, we are not able to engage with the KINGDOM realm and dimension of God. Our spirit man, who was dead because of the fall, can't even see this realm and KINGDOM world of God. Therefore we need to be born again spiritually by the breath of God to see, enter, dwell, and operate in the KINGDOM of God. Once our newly born again spirit becomes mature, we grow to see, feel, taste, smell, and hear the KINGDOM of God. The more we see and hear of the KINGDOM of God, the less we fall victim to the "world" and illusion that the enemy is using to deceive the masses. To be born again is definitely a KINGDOM weapon to overcome the world. You have to be born again to see the KINGDOM to overcome the world by tapping into a new heaven to birth a new earth.

The Weapon of Faith

Another weapon that works side by side with being born again to overcome the world is the KINGDOM weapon of faith. Is not one of the components of the armor of God, the shield of faith? The word faith in the Greek is the word "pistis" and this word means persuasion. To be born again to see the KINGDOM of God, you first must hear the word (gospel) of the KINGDOM and then be persuaded by that word of the KINGDOM enough to repent. This persuasion (faith) and repentance allows for Christ to come into your heart and the breath of God to re-birth you.

Faith (persuasion) comes from hearing and hearing by the word of God. You hear the word of God, and faith comes with that Word. You are persuaded which gives opening for faith to find a home within you which causes you to believe in your heart and confess with your mouth. You believe therefore you speak your confession. We call this saving faith. Even though we are saved by grace, we are saved and born again by faith.

This saving faith in conjunction with being born again causes you to see and enter the KINGDOM of God. And this faith is not a one time thing that operates in the beginning but throughout your whole KINGDOM journey. This is why Christ is the author and finisher of our faith. Everything in the KINGDOM of God operates by faith. Faith is so powerful that faith the size of a mustard seed, which is one of the least of seeds, can move mountains and do other incredible things. Faith is so important that we are told that without faith we can't please God the King. We definitely need faith to align with the King and defeat the enemy.

In Hebrews 11, which we call the faith hall of fame, faith is the "substance" of things hoped for and the "evidence" of things not seen. Faith allows you to peek in the realm of the KINGDOM of God and see things that are already established from the foundation of the world. There was a foundation before the world was created which is the Word and the will of God. This supersedes the world and the illusion of the enemy because it is the foundation and was there before. With faith we see the things of God and his KINGDOM and now can "hope" for them and declare them by faith. The word "substance" means reality. The KINGDOM realm of God is real, alive, and tangible and you can see this realm by faith.

Faith is not only the substance of things hoped for. But is also the evidence or witness of things not seen by your physical eyes. Faith means you are looking through new spiritual eyes. (I am not talking about the demonic counterfeit of the third eye.) You are not going by what you see physically but what your spirit man is receiving and seeing from the realm of the KINGDOM of God. You are now an eye-witness by the gift of faith that God has given you. The key is to use the gift of faith as a weapon against the enemy. That which is before and that which was established from the beginning which has the foundation of the Word of God overcomes the enemy every time.

A person can have a gun with bullets but if they don't pull the trigger then it means nothing. Another person can have a bow and arrow but if they don't put that arrow in the bow and draw back that bow to release the arrow, their warfare or hunting will be futile. I say this to show that faith as a weapon has to be activated and released. We know that faith is a weapon because the KINGDOM believer is told to fight the good fight of faith.

You have to activate faith as a weapon with your mouth. When you received Christ, even though you believed in your heart, you still had to release your faith by confessing with your mouth. Every aspect of faith must be activated by your decree and your actions since faith without works is dead.

Through faith *we understand that* **the worlds were framed by the word of God**, *so that* **things which are seen were not made of things which do appear**. *(Hebrews 11:3)*

From the above verse, we see that God has faith and through faith he framed the worlds he created by the words he spoke. And by speaking, the things which were in the invisible KINGDOM realm manifested into the visible realm. This is why faith is so powerful. When we can see by faith that which is of the KINGDOM of God and release with our mouth the Word of God to frame a new world, we can manifest the KINGDOM of God. Then the "world" of the enemy will crumble and the KINGDOM of God will expand and increase. As my wife likes to say a lot, "Faith is a moving thing". I agree, faith is a moving weapon when activated can take territories for the glory of the KINGDOM of God. Work that faith!!!!

Overcoming The Flesh

*For if ye live after the flesh, ye shall die: but if ye **through the Spirit** do mortify the deeds of the body, ye shall live. (Romans 8:13)*

We have discussed how to overcome the enemy and the world. Now let's talk about the third area we need to overcome. There is the enemy and his operating system "the world" but he needs a people who operate and live in his system of sin and death. The enemy is looking for people who live by the flesh. The flesh is the third area that we need to overcome. The flesh is the carnal nature that resides in fallen mankind. The fall of Adam and Eve kicked off a chain reaction where the divine nature of God which was the in image of God was stripped and the carnal nature was the residual state of man.

The flesh is the nature where man feels he can do anything he wants and that he is brilliant and beautiful on his own account. The flesh has an aspect where it wants to live by the dictates of the five senses of the body. The flesh causes man to lust after sinful pleasures and not seek the direction and kingship of God. The flesh is the combination of a carnal mind and the body living without the breath and inspiration of God. The flesh is at enmity with God and therefore the enemy of God.

Operating in the flesh is the opposite of Proverbs 3:5,6 where a man leans to his own understanding, directs his own steps, and doesn't trust in God at all. When I think of the flesh, I think about what King David said in Psalms 51 when he declared that he was shaped in iniquity and in sin he was conceived. It is for this state that Christ came to redeem mankind because in our flesh dwells no good thing. Also, there is not any way that we can function in our KINGDOM capacity through the carnal flesh.

God's intention was for the spirit man of a man joined as one with the Holy Spirit to be king, the soul to be the servant, and the body to be slave to the spirit man. The intention of the enemy is to have that pyramid upside down where the body and him is king. When God's intention is at play, an individual is operating in the KINGDOM of God. But when the body and all its desire is king, then that individual is operating in the flesh. The carnal mind versus the spiritual mind. This dynamic is so critical that Apostle Paul in Romans chapter 7 shared that when he wanted to do good, evil (the flesh) was present. He continues to say that he realized that there was a law that works in the members of his body. This perplexed him so much that he says" what wretched man am I?". The flesh, if given license, will take the driver seat everytime and must be overcome by KINGDOM believers.

The Weapon of the Holy Spirit

For the flesh lusteth against the Spirit, and the Spirit against the flesh: and these
are contrary the one to the other: (Galatians 5:17)

The reason the flesh must be overcome is because flesh and blood will not inherit the KINGDOM of God (1 Corinthians 15). If flesh is trying to reign in your life, then this prohibits KINGDOM fullness in your life. According to Galatians 5:17, the flesh and the Spirit are always at war and contrary to one another. This is why the obvious way to overcome the flesh is by the Holy Spirit. Christ came to baptize us with the Holy Spirit and from Acts 1:8 we know that after that the Holy Spirit comes upon us, we shall receive power. More than just being born again by the Holy Spirit, we need to be filled and baptized with the power of the Holy Spirit. It is this power that will be a weapon against the flesh and the enemy.

We need God's Holy Spirit power. We need a relationship with the Holy Spirit so he can comfort us against the enemy and instruct us in wisdom. The spirit of man is the candle of the Lord and when the Holy Spirit is joined to our spirit that candle is lit with the fire of God to translate us from the KINGDOM in darkness to the KINGDOM of marvelous light. A flesh led life leads to darkness and death but a Spirit led life leads to life and light. The identifying mark of a mature son of the KINGDOM of God is that they are led by the Spirit of God per Romans 8:14.

*For if ye live after the flesh, ye shall die: but if ye **through the Spirit** do mortify the deeds of the body, ye shall live. (Romans 8:13)*

The weapons that we use against the enemy are not carnal but mighty through God. So the carnal mind and the carnal flesh will not bring us victory against the enemy nor will it advance us in the KINGDOM of God. We need the Holy Spirit which will arm us with the full armor of God to provide with us the helmet of salvation. And by the Spirit of truth, we will be girded in our loins with truth. Also, the Holy Spirit will teach us to utilize the sword of the Spirit, the Word of God, properly. The more we yield to the Holy Spirit, the flesh will succumb to defeat. Romans 8:13 lets us know that through the Holy Spirit, the deeds of the flesh will be mortified (brought to death). Oh Holy Spirit, how we need you.

The whole chapter of Galatians 5 provides expertise in this area. One verse lets the reader know that if you don't want to fulfill the desires of the flesh, you must walk in the Spirit. To me, to walk in the Spirit means to live, breathe, move, and have your being in the KINGDOM realm of God. Prayer, worship, the Word, fasting, and praise are some of the vehicles that transport you to "walk in the spirit". Also, there are two paths and proofs if you are being led by the Holy Spirit. The Holy Spirit produces visible fruit in your life but the list of "works of the flesh" in Galatians 5 is a guideline if you are functioning in the flesh.

The Holy Spirit is a friend to us. The Holy Spirit intercedes on our behalf. The Holy Spirit warns us and at times might rebuke us so we can get back in line. The Holy Spirit points to and reminds us all truth. The Holy Spirit has his own gifts like tongues, prophecy, word of wisdom, word of knowledge, working of miracles, gifts of healing, faith, and discerning of spirits. These gifts provide a great arsenal to combat and overcome the enemy and your flesh. Walk in the spirit!!!

Overcoming The Law of Sin and Death

Moreover the law entered, that the offence might abound. But where sin abounded, grace did much more abound: (Romans 5:20)

In the first chapter of the Gospel of John, there is a scripture that proclaims that the law came by Moses but grace and truth came by Jesus Christ the Messiah. This scripture points to the fourth area that needs to be overcome which is the law of Moses which is the law of sin and death. The notion that the law of Moses was not enough is solidified. There was a need for Jesus to bring something more substantial and potent on the scene was the solution for this lack. The law of Moses is in part with types and shadows whereas Christ is the fullness. The law of Moses is holy but not perfect to bring us as believers to perfection. Condemnation, sin, and death is the byproduct of the law of Moses.

In Romans 5:20 (previously featured), when the law of Moses comes, its purpose is to expose and put emphasis on the offense of the law. It is through the law of Moses where sin is identified and we know that the wages of sin is death. So if there is a system where laws and ordinances are in place to identify sin, then death will be the punishment and verdict if we miss the mark of the law. And one thing about the law of Moses is that if you are guilty of one part, you are guilty of it all. But Christ came to blot out the ordinances that were against us and set up a government that we can serve God by not trying to follow some rules through the will of our flesh. But now through Christ, we can honor him by a renewed spirit and nature. Therefore, we can now be the Sons of God.

With this law of Moses that exposes sin, then the enemy actually uses this to be the accuser of the brethren. The enemy is very legalistic because the KINGDOM of God is a government that operates in KINGDOM laws. Did you know that there are courts in heaven where the enemy is going to make accusations against you? For those who don't know their rights in the new covenant and for those who choose not to live in the KINGDOM of God and grace, then the law of Moses will be your enemy.

In the book of Hebrews, the reader knows that during the reading of Moses, a veil is fitted over our heart making us not to fully see the full glory of God. The law of Moses is a ministry of death where the new testament and covenant is a ministry of life and peace. Where the law of Moses is, sin and death are close by because the law of Moses is weak through the flesh. Where sin abounds, grace and truth much more abounds. The goal is for us to use the weapons of grace and truth to overcome the law of Moses and death.

The Weapon of Grace

*For sin shall not have dominion over you: for **ye are not under the law, but under grace**. (Romans 6:14)*

In the second chapter of Ephesians, the bible lets the readers know that we are saved by grace through faith. And through grace which is the gift of God we are not saved by ourselves but we are actually God's workmanship. Grace works along with faith so that we can be the manifested image of God's workmanship. Grace is a very important component to our salvation and us entering fully into the KINGDOM of God.

There is a lot of talk about the mercy of God and the grace of God and some even look at it as the same thing. But actually they are two sides of the same coin of God which is his gift to mankind. Mercy is us not getting what we deserve while grace is us getting that which we don't deserve. One holds back the bad from us and the other one gives the good that God desires to give us. Some might say grace is God's unmerited favor. But it is so much more. It is not just his favor but it is God working in you by his Spirit. The Holy Spirit is the spirit of grace. So the definition that has been given me by revelation is that grace is the supernatural endowment of God working and living in you to do the will of God. That is why man can't boast, because for us to overcome, it has to be all him and by him. It is God who works in us to will and to do. This is the true grace of God.

Who knew that the gift of God of grace was more than a gift but actually a weapon to cause us to triumph. Some misuse the mercy of God by thinking that grace is a get out of free card but in reality grace is God's ace in his pocket to guarantee victory in our lives. To whom much is given , much is required. The Father did not send his Son to die on the cross for us just so we can do whatever our flesh wants. And so that everything will be all good for us while we still live a life riddled with sin. No, Christ died so his Spirit can live in us and work in us so we can do the works of Christ. Shall we continue in sin so that grace may abound? God forbid.

Salvation is not about our works from our own will and fleshly desires or us trying to pretend to be perfect. But it is about the grace of God bringing us unto "good works" (Ephesians 2). When we truly operate in the grace of

God and let it be all God we transcend from the law of Moses into the realm of faith which brings us under the constitution of the KINGDOM of God. We overcome the law and its judgment with the endless supply of the grace of God.

The mercies and grace of God are new every morning and we must come boldly to the throne of grace to find help in our time of need. We need him every hour and every day. We must live off the supply of his grace every day. We are like cars that need fuel. We can't let our tank go empty. We need to seek the throne of grace and the presence of God to be fueled everytime to win against the enemy. His grace will cause us to rise above sin and death, and to live in a new and living way which is not by the law of Moses, the law of sin and death. No KINGDOM believer can ever be an overcomer without the weapon of grace.

The Weapon of Truth (the law of the spirit of life)

*1 There is therefore **now no condemnation** to them which are in Christ Jesus, who walk not after the flesh, but after the Spirit. 2 For **the law of the Spirit of life in Christ Jesus** hath **made me free** from **the law of sin and death**.*
(Romans 8:1-2)

We just discussed briefly about the power of the weapon of grace. But this weapon works in combination with the weapon of truth. Truth is revealed biblically by the Word of God, a law, and by the Spirit of God. I want to clarify something that you might think I am saying but I am NOT.. I am not saying that having the "law" in place is bad. I am also not saying that the law of Moses is bad because it is the school master that was in place until the truth is revealed in our hearts. I am saying that the law of Moses is weak through the flesh but Christ has brought another law, which is the law of the KINGDOM of God, that is strong by the Spirit of God. There are two laws and one is greater than the other by far. There are two laws, one serves death and the other one serves life. That is why people who were righteous and died before Christ came were not able to rise to the highest heaven after they died. They ended up in Sheol in Abraham's bosom across a fixed gulf where on the other side were people who were dealing with torment on some level. The law of sin and death (Moses) was not able to bring the fullness of life in a person.

You might be wondering what "the truth" has to deal with all this law talk. Well simply put, the truth is the law of the spirit of life. This law of sin and death we must overcome to put on truth. We need the spirit of grace to lead us to all truth. Christ is the way, the truth, and the life. Christ told us that the Holy Spirit will speak of Christ and lead us into all truth. So the Holy Spirit who is also the spirit of grace will lead us out of the bondage of the law of Moses into a new law of the Spirit of life that is by Christ Jesus. Do you see the progression? We are called from the law of Moses (sin and death) by Christ (the way) through the Holy Spirit (grace) into truth and life.

It is all by Christ who when he came on the scene spoke of greater things than what the law of Moses could fully convey. This is why the Pharisees and those of the law were confounded and at awe because he spoke with such authority. He is the Way, the Truth, the Word, and the Life. The words of the enemy are not the truth. The natural world, that some might call an illusion, is not the truth but Christ and his words are the truth (the law of the Spirit of life). For Christ's words are spirit and life. The way to operate in the weapon of truth is to abide in Christ and his words abide in you. Truth is a perspective that you only see through the lens of Christ. Truth is the full reality of seeing things through the same perspective of the Father and his Son the Christ.

Truth is another realm. It is another territory and dimension of the KINGDOM that is spiritual. To bring this home, in John the 4th chapter, a woman asked Christ which physical mountain they should worship at. But Christ's response was something interesting. He did not pick a physical place. He told her that the time is coming and even "now" where those who worship the Father will worship him "in spirit and in truth". I am here to tell you that true worship is not achieved at a physical place but when you worship, love, and serve God from a pure heart (truth) that translates you to a place in the spiritual realm in Christ. Living in the fullness of Christ with all your heart, mind, soul and strength will be a weapon to have you reign over the law of sin and death. And walking and living in the realm of spirit and truth will make you free from any snares of the enemy and death. The TRUTH will make you free and who the SON has freed is free indeed. The truth will shut down the Father of lies and his accusations every time.

The Mighty Weapon of the Name of Jesus Christ (Yeshua)

*9 Wherefore God also hath highly exalted him, and **given him a name** which **is above every name**: 10 That **at the name of Jesus every knee should bow**, of things in heaven, and things in earth, and things under the earth; 11 And that every tongue should confess that Jesus Christ is Lord, to the glory of God the Father. (Philippians 2:9-11)*

I started the chapter by looking at certain things we as KINGDOM believers need to overcome and the weapons that will overcome those specific areas but I want to conclude with one more mighty weapon, the name of Christ. The Father has given Christ a name which is above every name. It is not just some names but every name is under the dominion of Christ. This name that is above all names signifies that Christ is KING and has a KINGDOM. So when we use the name of Christ Jesus (Yeshua), we are declaring the authority of a KINGDOM. We are called to walk in KINGDOM authority by using his name.

I want to note that using the name is not about using some "magic" word in any given situation. But when you look up the word "name" in Hebrew and Greek, it is more than just some letters or a word you call something by. There is a spiritual component to that name because the word "name" implies nature and characteristics. Usually when a name is used it has a certain brand or spiritual nature that it aligns with. I say all this to say that if you are not operating in the new divine nature of God by being born again, then just repeating the name of Christ will not mean a thing. Because as we declare the name, we are speaking to spiritual things and those spiritual things will see in the spirit if you have the spiritual capacity and components to legally utilize the name. The enemy and demons will bow to the KINGDOM image of Christ in you.

One way to see it is that the name is a family name. Ephesians 3:14-15 declares that with the name of the Father of the Lord Jesus Christ, that the whole family of God in heaven and earth is named by one name. So my family name is "Ellis" and with that name might come a certain reputation. If you are a KINGDOM believer, you are part of a family name and this name will grant you access to certain areas and give you clout against any opponent. There is power in the family name of Jesus Christ (Yeshua). This name is a weapon.

Another perspective besides the family perspective, is for you to see that you are part of a KINGDOM. And the King has made some decrees that stand throughout his full KINGDOM. And you have been in the presence of the KING. He has given you verdicts, judgments, scrolls, prophecies, promises, and the list goes on. He has put the seal of his name on you and made you an ambassador of the KINGDOM to go into new territories to proclaim the decrees of the KINGDOM of God. So when you use the weapon of the name of Christ as an ambassador of the KINGDOM, you have to know that you are backed by the whole of the KINGDOM of Heaven. The name of Christ when you operate in the nature of God and when you align to the KINGDOM agenda will be the weapon to bring all enemies to their knees. Know what and who you are!!!! It is a powerful thing to walk in the KINGDOM authority of the name of Christ!!!

Summary Chart

Areas To Overcome	Weapons To Use
The Enemy (Accuser)	Blood of the Lamb, The Word of God, The Love For God **[Revelation 12:11]**
The World (The Heaven, earth, sea)	Being Born of God, Faith **[1 John 5:4]**
The Flesh (The Inner Kingdom)	The Holy Spirit (Gifts & Fruit) **[Romans 8:13]**
The Law of Sin and Death (government)	Grace and Truth **[Romans 8:2 ; Romans 6:14]**

For every thing we need to overcome, the Most High has provided weapons for every threat and obstacle possible for the sake of his KINGDOM!!!

Chapter 12 : Change The Perspective

KINGDOM Fullness

*11 And he gave some, apostles; and some, prophets; and some, evangelists; and some, pastors and teachers; 12 For **the perfecting of the saints**, for the **work of the ministry**, for the edifying of the body of Christ: 13 **Till we all come in the unity of the faith**, and of the **knowledge of the Son of God**, unto **a perfect man**, unto **the measure of the stature of the fulness of Christ**:(Ephesians 4:11-13)*

It is the Father's will for us to walk in the fullness of his KINGDOM. In Ephesians 4, Christ Jesus (Yeshua) gave gifts to men in the form of KINGDOM apostles, prophets, evangelists, pastors and teachers. He released this to the body of Christ as he was ascending to the Father which is why I called these the KINGDOM ascension gifts. These gifts are to help bring the body to fullness, maturity, and perfection as well as teach them to overcome and ascend to the KINGDOM above to flow in the rightful positions as KINGDOM heirs.

In verse 12 it shows that these KINGDOM ascension gifts are for the perfecting of the saints so they can do their ministry (service) to help edify and build the body of Christ. I believe most who are claiming to be of the fivefold ministry gifts understand the part about edifying the body. But the goal of these leaders in the church as shown in verse 13 is to help mankind come into the unity of the faith to a knowing of the Son of God and to bring us to the full stature (fullness) of Christ. The first implication of this, is for the fivefold leadership of the body to be able to do this, they themselves must be at a level of KINGDOM maturity, holiness, and righteousness. We can only lead people to the level we have been.

Today, we see leaders who are not reflecting righteousness and living carnal lives where some have had scandals that promote to their congregants that it is acceptable to be lukewarm in their KINGDOM pursuit. This is not the will of the Father. He wants those who are of the fivefold KINGDOM ascension gifts to be at a level of KINGDOM engagement and intimacy with the Lord where they can mentor and edify the body of Christ. He wants them to walk in some level of KINGDOM fullness so they can lead others into fullness. As people go through the KINGDOM process, they will deal with the KINGDOM within, and begin to ascend and learn the KINGDOM above, and also operate as the KINGDOM flows through them. At that point of maturity, then Christ will commission them to help and lead others in that same process. The aim and goal should be KINGDOM fullness all around where everyone is conformed to the image and the fullness of the stature (height) of the Son.

In the topic of fullness, this is why we have to rise above the law of Moses because as the book of Hebrews conveys, the law of Moses along with the tabernacle and feasts, were types and shadows. It was not the full picture and it only showed things in part and not the fullness of the picture. Instead of going to a physical temple, we are the temples of the Holy Ghost on earth. And instead of the physical temple outlined in the Old Testament being the epitome of fullness, it points to the heavenly temple above. The feasts of the Lord speak of Christ. They symbolize our journey from Passover to Tabernacles as we go from repentance through the sacrifice of Christ to KINGDOM ascension and rest with the Father and Son. We are being called to leave the shadows, types, and that which is in part and to look for the real, the whole, and fullness of the KINGDOM. No more just following outward rules and commands of the letter. But it is time to walk in KINGDOM fullness by the Holy Spirit to see, enter, inherit, and enlarge the KINGDOM of the Most High.

The Higher Call

13 Brethren, ***I count not myself to have apprehended****: but this one thing I do,* ***forgetting those things which are behind****, and* ***reaching forth unto those*** ***things which are before****, 14 I press* ***toward the mark for the prize of the*** ***high calling of God in Christ Jesus****.(Philippians 3:13-14)*

I want to emphasize like Apostle Paul did in Philippians 3, in this journey towards KINGDOM fullness, I do not claim to have apprehended or arrived. I am very much on this journey and have a ways to go and so much more to learn and experience. Like Apostle Paul, the Most High have called some to be pioneers to announce that something is possible. He will give them glimpses and blueprints and say go and build this and announce this to the people. . And what I am doing in this book is to announce that the Most High has called us to a high calling and that high calling is the KINGDOM.

Here you have Apostle Paul writing many letters as an apostle of Christ and still saying that his goal is that he must press toward the mark for the prize.

Oh just because you are a part of the fivefold KINGDOM ascension gifts, you have not arrived and there is more to press towards. What prize is he referring to? The prize is the high calling of the Most High that can only be attained through Christ. And to get this prize, the KINGDOM, you have hit a certain mark or target. And what is that mark and where is that mark? The mark is Christ and the mark is in Christ. We have to find Christ and follow Christ. Remember one aspect of the KINGDOM is where the King is. The high calling which is our first call based on Romans 8:29 is to be conformed to the image of the Son. And the way to be conformed to the Son is to be where the Son is and become face to face with him so that you can be changed into the same "image" of what you are beholding (2 Corinthians 3:18).

The calling is not a low calling or regular calling, it is a high calling. We are being called up high where the Most High lives in the Highest of the Heavens. We are being called to come up hither and ascend to the holy hill of the Lord. The KINGDOM is a spiritual calling and we must continually have the mindset that we seek those things above as Colossians 3:1 encourages to. We can no longer make this Christian journey about just living in this physical realm and just trying to be good and be satisfied with that. The call and invitation is to engage the KINGDOM above if we truly want to walk in the high calling.

The high calling is not just about coming up high to take a tour of heaven and kick it with the angels, but the high calling is about relationship and responsibility. In the KINGDOM above as you press into the calling, it is about you knowing the Father and Christ in a new way. But the responsibility is that you are to be a mature Son as Christ is and walk in sonship as a King and Priest. The true reign as a King happens in the high places. And the high calling as a priest occurs in the Heavenly Temple. This is why it is the high calling because you have to function in a higher realm.

One principle of the KINGDOM is the principle of the Highest which basically declares that which has higher positioning has dominion over that which is lower. That is why Christ has caused us to sit together with him in heavenly places so we can truly reign above all principalities and powers. It is above and high that the image of Christ is solidified in us. The image begins within us but is perfected above. So we can't now just think of KINGDOM building from a carnal perspective or approach but the priority must be to press towards the high calling which is above. We have heard that which is born of spirit is spirit and that which is born of flesh is flesh. But that which is earthly minded will produce things that are earthly but we must be born of heaven to produce heaven in the earth.

The high calling is in Christ Jesus (Yeshua). We must abide in him, learn of him, follow him and his commandments. It takes a hard press to launch into this high calling which means it is not an automatic thing. It is not the easiest because you have to change from having an earthly and carnal mindset. You have an enemy who wants to stop you and is constantly trying to throw your past in your face. But to press into the high calling of the KINGDOM you have to forget those things behind and forget the failures and weaknesses of the past and press with all your heart, mind and strength for the sake of the high calling in Christ Jesus (Yeshua).

1 Wherefore seeing we also are compassed about with so great a cloud of witnesses, **let us lay aside every weight***, and* **the sin which doth so easily beset us***, and* **let us run with patience the race that is set before us***, 2* **Looking unto Jesus** **the author and finisher of our faith***; who for the joy that was set before him endured the cross, despising the shame, and* **is set down at the right hand of the** **throne of God***. (Hebrews 12:1-2)*

You have to die to self and decrease so you can increase in the things of Christ. To go high as the high calling requires, you have to lay aside every sin and weight that so easily snares you. The more weight on you, the more likely you can't jump that high or go that fast. This is what sin, distractions, and pleasures of this life do. It pulls and slows you down. Even airlines want to make sure that their airplanes have a certain weight so it can fly without any issues. We have to let go of everything that hinders our press for the mark of the high calling.

The high calling is in Christ and Christ is at the right hand of the throne of the Father which is the pinnacle of the KINGDOM. Hebrews 12:1-2 shows us that we are in a race that we have to run with patience. The finish line is far off and may take some time to get to it but the key is to continue to look at Christ. This is an indicator that the race leads you high and above because where you are supposed to look at is at the right hand of the Father above where Christ is seated. We as born again KINGDOM citizens are called to a high calling which is in Christ. May we heed the call so we can be the few that are chosen to be a part of the gathering and church of the firstborn which is in the KINGDOM above.

Summary

The book is lengthy and that is with me sharing things at a high level but there will be other books that will take deeper dives in the future. This book is more of an introduction that will lead to other KINGDOM topics but before we can understand the rest we must get the basics and shift to the KINGDOM perspective and mindset. The KINGDOM is quite the topic and it is vast and we probably can write or read a thousand books and it would not include everything. Our Heavenly Father has no limits and his KINGDOM has no end so there is much that can be discussed. But in the section, I just wanted to hit some high level points that you should walk away with after reading this book.

- **What is the KINGDOM?:** The KINGDOM of the Most High is the rule and reign of the Most High and Christ **in you**, **above or over you**, and **through you** with the intention to be all in all.
- **Image First:** It is the image of Christ that is our first call and this is the image you need to rule and have dominion in the KINGDOM.
- **War over the Territory:** The KINGDOM of the Most High is about domains and territories and there is an enemy who wants the same territories that the Most High desires. Hence, there is a war going on in certain territories.
- **It's all about the KINGDOM:** The intention of the Father as expressed from Genesis to Revelation is all about his KINGDOM and those who will be part of his royal bloodline.
- **Gospel of the KINGDOM:** And because it's all about the KINGDOM, Christ and his disciples proclaimed the good news of the KINGDOM. The gospel must be announced and proclaimed with a message to call people to repentance because the KINGDOM is here, near, and now.
- **Seek The KINGDOM First:** The first priority after believing the gospel of the KINGDOM and responding with repentance is to seek the KINGDOM of the Most High within you.
- **The KINGDOM Now:** The KINGDOM is no more at hand. It is closer than that. The KINGDOM is Here and now ready for you to seek so you can see, enter, inherit and enlarge the KINGDOM
- **Progression of the KINGDOM:** The KINGDOM of the Most High must start deeper within you to lead you Higher to the KINGDOM above so you can then bring that which is higher lower to advance the KINGDOM forward. This is how the KINGDOM flows through you.
- **The KINGDOM Within You:** The KINGDOM within is Christ taking total possession of your heart, mind, soul, strength (might), and your tongue. Christ wants to sit on the throne of your heart so that life can be in the power of your tongue.
- **The KINGDOM Above You:** The KINGDOM above requires that we must ascend to this realm that includes the Heavenly Jerusalem, the Holy Mt. Zion, The Father, Christ, a company of angels, and even the courts

and councils of heaven. In this realm is the royal priesthood after the order of Melchizedek where we function as kings and priests.

- **The KINGDOM Through You:** With engagement and involvement with the KINGDOM Above, then you can be used to decree the KINGDOM to come so that the will of heaven can become reality on the earth. That which is above will become below through you as you manifest as a mature son of the KINGDOM on the earth.
- **Called To Overcome:** We have the enemy, the world, the flesh, and the law of Moses to overcome. The call of sonship is to overcome these things and inherit (possess) the KINGDOM given to us of our Heavenly Father.

Change The Perspective

The perspective of the gospel that is being preached in most mainstream churches across the world has to change. It has to be more than Christ died for your sins and now your sins can be forgiven. It has to be more than if you live right, then you can go to heaven when you die. It has to be more than let's wait for Christ to crack the sky before we even think about the KINGDOM. It has to be more than about people repeating after you to do a confession of Christ so they can be on your member roll or a number in your statistics of how many you converted to Christ. Something has to change if we want to walk in the more that the Father has said we can walk in.

It can't be about just getting converts and church members but it has to be about KINGDOM discipleship. The message must be the gospel of the KINGDOM and teaching must be about seeing, entering, inheriting and enlarging that KINGDOM. Christ has to be introduced as more than a merciful savior who comes along and cleans all your messes. This is just part of it. He is forgiving your sins so he can cleanse you from all unrighteousness within you so you can have access to the KINGDOM. He is more than a Savior, but he is Lord and King. He is King of a KINGDOM that has no end and he wants you to be a part of the KINGDOM not as a servant but as a Son to the Father. Our message has to change and our perspective has to change.

The perspective has to change because it impacts everything downstream. When the message is watered down or the message of the KINGDOM is omitted, then we don't walk in KINGDOM fullness and make the KINGDOM the priority to seek it first. We don't realize that there are qualifications for the KINGDOM and so there is no urgency to lay down everything for the KINGDOM and press into it. When we keep Christ and his KINGDOM top of mind, it will impact what and how we preach. It will impact how we teach, shepherd, and disciple people. It will impact even how you walk in power, authority and glory because this is what the KINGDOM is. It will cause people to strive for righteousness, peace and joy because this is what the KINGDOM is all about.

When the KINGDOM is preached and proclaimed from the beginning, it sets the mark and target. Expectations are realized from the start. We see that the aim is to be like Christ and we see that we need to press towards the mark of the high calling of the KINGDOM which is Christ Jesus (Yeshua). So when the perspective is changed, the expectations and the goal are different which cause a different urgency and obedience. There is a different reverence and obedience when you just look at the Most High as a savior instead of looking at him as a savior AND King. The message of the KINGDOM and that perspective holds nuances of sonship, priesthood, and kingship that has been made available to us. Salvation just to go to heaven when you die minimizes the fullness of the KINGDOM that we can walk in while we live here now on the earth. The perspective must shift to the KINGDOM of the Most High.

The Father has great things in store for us and he is calling the body to align back to the KINGDOM perspective. This is his original intention and the body of Christ has put other things ahead of the KINGDOM. Christ and his KINGDOM must be the central theme in all we say and do. It is time to change the perspective. The KINGDOM of the Most High is here, near, and right now. It is all about the KINGDOM!!! Our words, our actions, our motives must be aligned to the KINGDOM and what the King desires. We must eat, sleep, dream, and talk about "KINGDOM, KINGDOM, and more KINGDOM". We must keep all things KINGDOM and shift to the KINGDOM perspective.

Invitation to the KINGDOM

You might not know the Lord Jesus Christ (Yeshua) as King and want to surrender to the King. If that is you, the invitation to the KINGDOM and the King still holds. And For those who might have read this book and you are a believer but you have never really thought about the things from the KINGDOM perspective, I have something for you. Below, is a prayer that can be utilized to accept the invitation to the KINGDOM of the Most High. It is just a template and guide. You can say it word for word or you can say it in your own words.

```
Heavenly Father, I believe in the gospel of the KINGDOM and that
your Son , Jesus (Yeshua) died on the cross for our sins and that
his blood blots out every record against me and now grants me
access to your KINGDOM. I repent from every sin, iniquity and I
turn to Christ as my Savior, Lord, and King in full obedience
with all my heart, mind and soul. Please breathe the breath of
the Holy Spirit within me so I can be born again of the Spirit to
see and enter the KINGDOM. Also, remove everything within me and
in my life that does not line up with your KINGDOM. I renounce
any other rulership of any demons and also renounce any illegal
```

and demonic covenants and curses. You are my King now and I want to be conformed to the image of your Son. Now I ask Father, give me the KINGDOM and cause me to see, enter, inherit, and enlarge the KINGDOM. Cause me to know you, my Heavenly Father and Christ your Son intimately according to John 17:3. I believe in the gospel of the KINGDOM and receive the KINGDOM by faith. I now declare that I am born again and on my way to embarking on the journey to be a mature Son in the KINGDOM of the Most High. In the name of your Son, Christ Jesus (Yeshua). So be it in my life. Amen.

Now go forth and take on the KINGDOM perspective and press forward to see, enter, inherit, and enlarge the KINGDOM of the Most High!!!!

About the Author

Dr. Martin Ellis, Jr. is a husband, father, songwriter, worshiper and author who has over 25 years of ministry experience as an apostolic and prophetic voice to the body of Christ. He is also known for his vibrant teaching style. He has served in areas of ministry such as prison ministry, youth pastor, worship leader, missions to Africa, and other leadership and mentoring capacities. Dr. Ellis' mandate is to help others find their destinies through the grace of God. Other aspects of his mandate is to shift the body of Christ to the kingdom of God perspective, demonstrate the power of God, introduce people to the glory of God, and equip believers and leaders to flow in the Kingdom of God. He is the founder of Open Face Glory International which is an outreach, internet ministry that brings focus to the kingdom, power, and glory of God. On the local level, he also is co-founder along with his wife, Prophetess LaRonda Ells, of Kingdom Fullness Ministries International which is a local assembly in the metropolitan St. Louis area. The heart of Dr. Ellis is to see the world know the supernatural working power of the Most High and see the whole earth filled with the glory of God. It is his desire for all to see Christ as King sitting on the throne of their hearts.

You can connect with me on:

- http://drmartinellisjr.com
- https://www.facebook.com/drmartinellisjr
- http://kingdom-fullness.org
- http://openfaceglory.org

Made in United States
Troutdale, OR
03/09/2024

18335517R00122